Chaos to Clarity

Estate Planning for People Who Think They Don't Need It

Maryam Greenidge

Maryam Greenidge

Chaos to Clarity
1st Edition, October 2025

Copyright © 2025 by Legal Code LLC

All rights reserved. No part of this publication may be reproduced, distributed, or transmitted in any form or by any means, including photocopying, recording, or other electronic or mechanical methods, without the prior written permission of the publisher, except in the case of brief quotations embodied in critical reviews and certain other noncommercial uses permitted by copyright law.

The scanning, uploading, and distribution of this book via the Internet or via any other means without the permission of the publisher is illegal and punishable by law. Please purchase only authorized electronic editions and do not participate in or encourage electronic piracy of copyrighted materials.

Disclaimer

This book is intended for informational and inspirational purposes only. The author and publisher make no representations or warranties regarding the accuracy, applicability, fitness, or completeness of the contents. The information provided is not a substitute for professional advice—readers should seek qualified counsel or expertise when appropriate. Neither the author nor the publisher shall be held liable for any loss or damages, including but not limited to indirect or consequential damages, arising from the use or reliance upon the material in this book. All names, characters, places, and incidents are used fictitiously unless otherwise stated. Any resemblance to actual persons, living or dead, events, or locales is entirely coincidental.

For permission requests, email: thelegalcodenyc@gmail.com

ISBN: 979-8-218-81727-5 (Paperback)
ISBN: 979-8-218-83957-4 (eBook)

Published in the United States of America

For my future children —
May you always know that you were dreamed of long before you arrived,
and that everything I have built was with you in my heart.

Table of Contents

Acknowledgments 6

Foreword 7

Introduction: Who Is This Book For? 9

Chapter 1: The Probate Trap and Why You Should Avoid It ... 18

Chapter 2: I Do Not Own Much—What Is the Value of a Trust for Me? 41

Chapter 3: How Irrevocable Trusts Impact Medicaid Long-Term Care Eligibility 59

Chapter 4: Plan for the Dreams You Chase and the Storms You Cannot See 78

Chapter 5: The Rest of the Story: Estate Planning Beyond Wills and Trusts 92

Chapter 6: A Debt to Remember: What Happens to Your Financial Commitments When You Are Gone? 99

Chapter 7: What Taxes Are Due When a Person Dies? 110

Chapter 8: The New American Dream: A Global Journey 124

Final Thoughts 135

Glossary of Terms 137

Appendix A: Sample Letter to Close Accounts 145

Appendix B: Sample Letter to Decedent's Employer and/or Administrator 147

Appendix C: Asset Preparation Worksheet 150

Acknowledgments

To my dearly departed grandparents Ivan and Sheila Savory—your spirit lives on in every page of this book.

To my parents, whose love and support have been the foundation of everything I have accomplished.

To my brother, your example continues to inspire me every day.

To Joel, thank you for your unwavering love and encouragement.

To my dearest sisters, Nana and Serwah, your love and support have been a steady light in my life.

To Esther, I cherish you as a sister and a friend. You have always stood in my corner.

To Carol, Harriet and Sandra, thank you for walking beside me on this journey.

To Kibibi, your inspiration and support have carried me through countless moments, and I am forever thankful.

Mina Irfan, you inspired me to play on the edge and reach beyond comfort — a gift I will always cherish.

Finally, to David Waller — thank you for changing the trajectory of my life. You opened doors that shaped my career, and for that, I am eternally grateful.

Foreword

Maryam is a native New Yorker. I am a San Francisco native. Despite living on opposite sides of our country, fate would still lead us to our friendship. We met during the pandemic inside a virtual village of high-achieving women being coached by Mina Irfan.

After following one another on social media, and sharing lighthearted conversations there, Maryam asked if we could exchange phone numbers. We initially chatted mostly about legal matters—as Maryam is an attorney, and I had been working in the legal profession a couple of decades by that time.

Then we discussed our personal lives.

During those thousands of hours over the phone, what was immediately uncovered is our core common value: HELPING OTHERS, and the deep fulfillment we get from sharing from our overflow.

I also pleasantly discovered that Maryam has what I like to call a *Teacher's Heart*. This is beautifully displayed on her YouTube channel (*The Legal Code*), where she pours out hours of FREE advice on legal topics, moving abroad, foreign policies, and cultural topics she studies and is passionate about.

In this book, Maryam offers invaluable Estate Planning insights — from an attorney's experience — in easily digestible ways for the masses. This sets Maryam far apart from the *billable hour* business model commonly used in the legal profession.

Maryam offers her heart and intellect from a genuine desire to simplify the overwhelming Estate Planning process (*customarily thought to be utilized only by the elite*), making it more accessible to you, your family, and future heirs.

Kibibi Shaw, MSOD

Introduction:
Who Is This Book For?

Very often, we hear the tragic stories where a loved one dies, and what should be a time of mourning turns into turmoil, conflict, and unanswered questions. Is there a Will or is there no Will? Or perhaps there are whispers of one hidden, lost, or never signed, but no one knows for sure. During a time of grief, families find themselves paralyzed, staring at a labyrinth of legal hurdles, lacking guidance, clarity, and peace. With no clear guidance and limited resources, the estate becomes mired in the probate process, dragging on for years. What should have been a time of healing and acceptance, turns into a prolonged struggle—draining energy, straining relationships, and leaving painful questions unresolved…

"Why didn't he plan ahead?"

"Why did he leave us this mess?"

"How could something so important be left to chance?"

These unanswered questions fester, transforming grief into a storm of chaos and endless what-ifs—leaving behind only pain, frustration, and a legacy no family deserves.

While families grapple with loss, opportunists emerge. Estranged relatives or acquaintances suddenly appear to claim money and possessions. They prey on the vulnerability of the grieving, scavenging for anything of value: vehicles, televisions, jewelry, clothing—anything not secured becomes fair game to take. The family, already struggling to cope with the loss, find themselves battling not only the complexities of probate and legal uncertainty but also the family members who exploit their misfortune.

This turmoil stems not just from the absence of a Will, but from the broader failure to organize one's affairs. Whether through missing documents, conflicting documents, or a complete lack of planning, the resulting chaos leaves permanent scars on grieving families.

I have spoken with countless people who, even after years of a loved one's passing, are still entangled in unfinished legal affairs—often because they did not know where to start or could not afford a lawyer to guide them. Therefore, I wrote this book as a practical guide for families to begin preparing. This estate planning guide is designed for everyday individuals and families. No legal jargon and no daunting processes—simply clear, helpful, and accessible information.

You may be thinking, "Estate planning? I do not even have an 'estate,' so this does not apply to me—that is something out of the *Downton Abbey* series or for a rich, aristocratic family." It is a common misconception for people to underestimate their value. Many hardworking people believe that estate planning is only for the wealthy to pass down their riches to their heirs. The truth could not be further from this notion. If you own a vehicle, a bank account, a few valuable collectibles, or a retirement fund—

no matter the balance—you do in fact have an estate. In simple terms, your estate includes everything you own: property, personal belongings, financial accounts, and debts.

Understanding what makes up your estate is the first step to recognizing why planning for it matters. As estate planning ensures these pieces of your life (think health, intellectual property, real estate, financial assets, and physical possessions) are managed and passed on according to your wishes. By understanding and organizing these elements, you take control of how your legacy is preserved. Therefore, the pages ahead show how estate planning becomes one of the most empowering steps you take, no matter your net worth.

Estate planning is a proactive process where you organize and manage your assets to ensure they are distributed according to your wishes after you pass away. It also prepares you for scenarios where you might become unable to make decisions due to illness or injury. Through estate planning, you establish legal protections, specify your preferences for medical, financial, and personal matters, and help your loved ones avoid difficult decisions. A well-crafted estate plan can also reduce taxes and preserve more wealth for future generations.

So, let us dispel the myth that estate planning is only for the wealthy or elderly. Whether you are signing your first lease or retiring debt-free, these decisions protect your family's future and your independence. But when these important steps are overlooked, the consequences can be far-reaching. Without a plan:

- A medical crisis could lead to legal battles over your care.
- Even small assets like a savings account or car could be tied up in probate for months.
- Your wishes—from healthcare to inheritance—may be ignored.
- Your heirs could face taxes when they inherit.
- No one may know where your assets are, or what you owned, risking them being claimed by the state.
- Liens could be placed on your home and accounts.

Therefore, estate planning is not merely wise; it is essential to ensuring you leave a personalized legacy instead of chaos. People cannot afford to ignore the importance of estate planning or delay action any longer. Fortunately, social media has played a key role in spreading awareness about estate planning and has, in a way, "democratized" this knowledge.

Here are additional benefits of estate planning:

(1) It is a tool for saving on taxes;

(2) It teaches future generations how to handle, leverage, and grow their inherited assets;

(3) It can help protect assets to qualify for Medicaid Long-Term Care;

(4) It helps build wealth and financial security for the next generation;

(5) It prevents assets from being used as collateral for long-term care;

(6) It minimizes or eliminates the need for probate, saving time, money, and emotional stress for your loved ones;

(7) It offers safeguards for minors, individuals with disabilities, or beneficiaries facing financial challenges;

(8) From healthcare decisions to distributing personal belongings, estate planning gives you control when you are unable to speak for yourself.

While the practical benefits are clear, the deeper purpose of estate planning is often overlooked. At its heart, estate planning is more than documents or decisions; it is an act of faith, love, and intention. Estate planning *is* about family—an expression of love that protects them, affirming your faith in their future, and extending your care long after you are gone. It is also about legacy, ensuring that the values and principles that guided your life continue to shape the lives of those who follow.

Additionally, beyond the legal lens, it also embodies religious, sacred, and spiritual principles. Many spiritual traditions emphasize that we are *caretakers*, not owners, of our resources, and that we must organize our affairs accordingly. The Holy Bible does not explicitly mention "estate planning," but it addresses themes such as wise stewardship, inheritance, legacy, family provision, and preparedness—all key elements of estate planning. Scripture frequently emphasizes stewardship, legacy, inheritance, and providing for loved ones. The book of Proverbs especially offers wisdom that aligns closely with these values:

Proverbs 13:22 (ESV): "A good man leaves an inheritance to his children's children, but the sinner's wealth is laid up for the righteous."

1 Timothy 5:8 (ESV): "But if anyone does not provide for his relatives, and especially for members of his household, he has denied the faith and is worse than an unbeliever."

Islam also highlights estate planning, considering it a spiritual and religious duty. The Holy Qur'an and Hadith provide clear guidance on wealth distribution after death, and following these rules is seen as obedience to Allah. Creating a Shariah-compliant will is considered an act of *taqwa* (God-consciousness), reflecting a Muslim's desire to obey Allah in death and protect family from conflict.

Surah Al-Baqarah (2:180): "It is prescribed for you, when death approaches [any] of you—if he leaves wealth—that he should make a bequest for the parents and near relatives, according to what is acceptable—a duty upon the righteous."

"And to all We have appointed heirs to what is left by parents and relatives. And to those whom your oaths have bound [to you]—give them their share. Indeed, Allah is ever, over all things, a Witness" (Qur'an 4.33, Saheeh International).

Jewish teachings also stress the importance of estate planning for maintaining *shalom bayit* (peace in the home). In Judaism, estate matters can directly impact harmony within the family. The story in Genesis 27 about Jacob and Esau's conflict over their father's blessing illustrates how unclear inheritance can cause division: "Esau said, 'Is he not rightly named Jacob? For he has cheated me these two times. He took away my birthright, and behold, now he has taken away my blessing'" (Gen. 27.36, ESV). Isaac's blessing was a form of spiritual estate, and the lack of clarity and favoritism caused a rupture between brothers. This example shows that estate planning is more than practical—it is a form of worship, divine duty, and personal responsibility rooted in faith. Rabbis and Jewish ethicists use this passage to emphasize the moral and emotional consequences of poor succession planning.

Building on this spiritual foundation, this book seeks to turn principles and faith into practice. It provides clear, actionable guidance to help you navigate the complex world of estate planning with confidence and intention. To that end, this book will prepare you to:

(1) Understand what is involved in estate planning and pitfalls to avoid
(2) Learn what probate is and how the process works

(3) Know what steps to take immediately after the death of a loved one
(4) Understand how to qualify for Medicaid Long-Term Care and maintain eligibility for other needs-based government programs
(5) Plan effectively for disabled or minor children
(6) Ensure your estate planning documents reflect your true wishes
(7) Understand how estate planning saves on taxes for succeeding generations
(8) Read and interpret a Will or Trust to confirm that your desires are clearly articulated
(9) Recognize the different uses of Trusts
(10) Explore the option of retiring abroad

These lessons are written with you in mind, especially if you have worked hard to build something meaningful and now wonder how to safeguard it. At its heart, this book is for those who want to leave behind more than assets—they want to leave a legacy of love, clarity, and security. To those readers, this book offers practical guidance tailored to their unique challenges. It speaks to first-generation property owners who worked tirelessly to build wealth yet remain unsure how to protect it. It supports immigrant families navigating the complexities of the American legal system, determined that their sacrifices translate into stability for future generations. It comforts those who lie awake at night wondering: *Will my family struggle when I am gone? Will my home be lost to probate or nursing home costs?* It also guides young parents who refuse to let their children inherit chaos, choosing instead to teach them how to steward wealth with wisdom. And it offers help to those with parents who resist thinking about estate planning, but who long for a way to start that conversation with care. Ultimately, this book is for every person who believes in building and preserving a legacy. If you believe your family deserves a roadmap rather than a mess, this book is your guide. Because true wealth is not merely what you leave—it is *how* you leave it.

With the goal of teaching you how to steward wealth with wisdom, this book has been structured as a practical resource, designed so that its chapters may be read independently and in any sequence. If you come across unfamiliar terms, a helpful "Glossary of Terms" is included to clarify key concepts. Please note that this book is not a substitute for professional legal advice, but a guide to help prepare you for informed conversations with a licensed practitioner in your area.

Chapter 1:
The Probate Trap and Why You Should Avoid It

Ask Yourself… *If something happened to you tomorrow, would your family know what to do?*

Imagine stepping into a state or local agency—the DMV, Social Security office, or maybe the Department of Vital Records. You have a straightforward task (or so you think) of filing a document. You arrive around 9:30 a.m. at a waiting area packed with people. A low murmur of voices echoes through the fluorescent-lit space. People wait in chairs, glancing at tickets or screens, eyes squinting with frustration as time drags. You notice a clerk shuffling papers, leaning back in a creaky office chair, with a mug of lukewarm coffee resting on her desk. She wears a tight, wrinkled blouse, paired with a knee-length skirt that is crooked on her hips and pilling from wear. You take note of her cluttered desk, full of faded yellow sticky notes. She types slowly, often pausing to dramatically sigh or yawn before continuing. Occasionally, she glances at a clock on the wall, appearing to count the minutes until lunch. When you approach her, she musters a bored response. You suddenly hear a ping of an email arriving. She tends to her computer screen, skimming it lazily, signaling that she will deal with it later.

Now, imagine this special brand of civil employee when one of your loved ones has passed away and you must organize their affairs with probate. Only, this clerk is stationed in a maze of filing cabinets, old records, and stacks of estate paperwork. She is seated behind a large, imposing dusty counter, surrounded by stacks of legal forms, file folders, and a desk fan slowly rotating despite the cold ambiance. When someone approaches her with questions about a loved one's case, she answers curtly: "You will need form 137B… I cannot help you without a death certificate… Processing time can be anywhere from three to six months, or longer." Her interactions are punctuated by long pauses as she retrieves documents or searches the system, eyes occasionally glazing over as she clicks through endless screens.

If the paperwork is incomplete, the clerk, in an indifferent tone, informs the family member that she will need to "return with all the necessary documentation." Her interactions lack urgency and empathy, showing no consideration for the family's grief or circumstances. In moments like these, what should be a compassionate exchange often turns into a cold encounter.

We have all had interactions and been handled by "this" civil servant. Such experiences leave families feeling frustrated, unseen, and alone at a time when they most need compassion. Is this what you want to leave your loved ones to have to experience in the wake of your death? Do you want this apathetic and uninterested clerk deciding the fate of your assets and your loved one's future? This is not purely a hypothetical concern—it is a reality many families face when the court system becomes the default decision-maker.

Furthermore, if your family is ever compelled to seek guardianship for you, they will probably be at the mercy of this type of public servant, who holds sway over the process that governs your care. And this lack of control extends beyond your care, reaching into the very future of your family's inheritance. Unless you create a clear plan for your assets, this special kind of bureaucrat—not you, and not your loved ones—will dictate how your life's work is divided. The painful task of navigating that outcome will fall squarely on your family's shoulders at the very moment they are least prepared to handle it.

The legal system itself acts as a barrier rather than a source of help, bound by rigid procedures that leave little room for compassion. It is designed to ensure fairness and order, relying on strict rules and guidelines to consistently manage estates. This structure often prioritizes protocol over compassion, which can make the process feel cold and impersonal—especially during such an emotional time for families.

Nowhere is this tension between order and empathy more visible than in the role of the probate clerk. The probate clerk is the gatekeeper, not a guide, tasked with following protocol and trained to be unempathetic. Probate clerks often have the reputation as being difficult—not because they are heartless—but because strict rules and legal limitations bind them. They are not permitted to give legal advice, interpret documents, or make exceptions, even when a grieving family is standing before them.

Their role is to ensure compliance with the law, not to simplify the process.

What is Probate?

This overwhelming burden stems from a process called probate. Probate is the state's court process of determining the rightful *heir* of a person's estate. An heir is the person legally entitled to inherit the property of another when a person dies. The law sees this person as entitled to inherit because he/she is related through blood or marriage. The state must determine who the heir is before any assets can be *distributed* or given out.

Even though it seems obvious that it is rather easy to determine lineage through birth certificates, marriage licenses, and orders of paternity, establishing lineage is still a complex process. This is especially true today because modern families are more dynamic and complicated than they have ever been historically. This complexity can be due to multiple marriages, siblings having different parents, out-of-wedlock births, unknown children, or unknown marriages. Therefore, the court relies on various verifying documents to determine who is the heir to an estate. Documents are required to determine lineage because the court does not know your family—it only knows what is on paper, and it uses those documents to decide who inherits your estate. One of the clearest ways to make sure the court is not left guessing or having to reconstruct a family tree from scattered documents is to create one clear, binding document: a *Last Will and Testament*.

Otherwise, without your direction, the court is left to assemble the pieces. A Will allows you to "speak" and declare your desires.

Will Power: Your Final Command

A *Last Will and Testament* (or simply a *Will*) is a legal document in which a person (called the *testator*) expresses their wishes regarding the *distribution* of their property and assets after their death. It can also specify guardianship for minor children, name an executor to carry out the Will's instructions, and provide other directions related to the estate. It is the official document that says who gets what, who takes care of things, and how a person's affairs should be handled after he/she dies.

When a person passes away with a Will, it must be submitted to the Probate Court or Surrogate's Court in the County in which the *decedent* (person who died) lived at the time of his/her passing. Therefore, having a Will does not help a family avoid probate because the Will has to be submitted to the court for verification. The Will is submitted along with additional documents that seek to verify the legitimacy of the Will and prove to the court that the Will reflects the decedent's desires. These documents are provided by the *petitioner* or the supporter of the Will, who says to the court, "*I want this Will to be entered and I support this Will as the decedent's last declaration of what he/she desired to be done with her properties and the nomination of the executor.*" The judge and county clerk look through the documents to determine whether the petitioner's case is sufficient to support the Will. If the court agrees and there is *no contest* (a person arguing against the validity of the Will) to the Will, then the court will issue *Letters of Testamentary*. These Letters are official documents that confirm that the court has accepted the Will and appointed the *executor,* or the person responsible for managing and settling the estate.

As you can see, even though a Will is a crucial document, it is not a surety to avoid probate because it must be submitted for verification. Despite its shortcomings, it at least gives the court and your family a roadmap. Without one, the process unravels into what is known as *intestate proceedings*.

The Chaos of an Unwritten Farewell (Intestate Proceedings)

Probate proceedings without a Will, legally referred to as an intestate proceeding, occur when the petitioner says to the court: *"the decedent died without a Will and without naming an heir, but we are asking the court to appoint this administrator to organize the estate of the decedent and distribute assets to beneficiaries because he/she are next of kin and should be selected based on marriage, intestacy law, or based on closeness in blood relation to the person who died."* Do you see how this can be problematic in many ways? Let us outline the reasons why this is undesirable through classic tales you already know:

(1) The Petitioner or administrator may not be who the decedent intended to handle their estate, but based on state

laws, he/she gets to ask the court to appoint him/herself because of close blood or marital relations.

    a. Example: *Cinderella's Dad wanted her to inherit his house and land but forgot to write a will, so her stepmother asks the court to appoint her as administrator of his estate.*

(2) There may be several people who are equally as close to the decedent based on blood relation, and each can also petition the court to request to be the executor or representative. For example, imagine that the decedent had three (3) children, each petitioning the court to be the administrator? Who should the court select?

    a. Example: *After the prince in Cinderella finds the glass slipper, several women claim to be the mysterious girl from the ball. Each step-sister believes she deserves to be chosen, and all seem equally eligible from the outside. However, only one truly fits the slipper, Cinderella.*

Similarly, if a decedent has three children, and all petition the court to serve as the administrator, the court must determine who "fits the slipper" best. This could depend on factors like who is most capable, or most impartial, or who has the support of the other heirs.

(3) People can claim to be an heir without being a legitimate heir.

    a. Example: *A princess kisses a frog who claims to be a prince—tall, charming, and heir to the throne. He insists, "Trust me, I am royalty!" Now, imagine this in an estate* case: *the court is reviewing heirs, and suddenly someone hops in (pun intended), croaks out a sad tale, and insists, "I am the long-lost child of the deceased!" But just like the frog, not everyone who says they are royalty (or an heir) is. The court, much like the skeptical princess, needs more than just a story. It wants proof—birth certificates, Wills, DNA tests—not just someone showing up and saying, "I am next in line!" So, until the "frog" proves he is really a prince, he is just a guy in a pond with good public relations.*

(4) The court must inquire and then notify all beneficiaries and interested family members about the death. This can take months or years to locate people because some may have moved, died, or become ill and, therefore, may be unaware or unavailable for this process.

    a. Example: *Think of Sleeping Beauty, when the king and queen throw a grand party to celebrate their daughter's birth, they invite all the important fairies in the land to bestow blessings. One fairy, who did not get the memo (or maybe did not update her mailing address), shows up late and furious. She was not invited because the castle staff could not find her. Now imagine the court is like the royal event planner. Before distributing the estate (or blessings), it must make sure that all the rightful heirs—the fairies of the family—are invited and notified. But like in the fairy tale, some heirs may be hard to find. They may have moved, changed names, passed away, or simply do not return calls. And if the court skips someone or sends notice to the wrong*

> *address, well... delays, disputes, and drama often follow. So, like any good kingdom, the court must conduct a full investigation before the magic—also known as the probate process—can begin.*

Based on these examples, you can see why dying without a Will is undesirable and causes so much uncertainty for the courts to resolve. It also leaves opportunities for bad actors to misrepresent in the hopes that they will inherit. Relatives may disagree over who gets what, leading to lengthy and costly legal battles that can strain relationships. Additionally, an intestate proceeding may incur higher legal fees, court costs, and taxes. The lack of clear instructions and the need for court involvement often result in higher expenses for beneficiaries.

A Will typically provides clarity by specifying how assets are to be shared amongst heirs, which can help prevent conflicts and is essential for avoiding the confusion of intestacy. However, Wills alone do not guarantee a smooth process. Wills also have complex procedures depending on the circumstances. Therefore, probate proceedings, even with a Will in place, frequently involve unexpected complications. As will be demonstrated in the following section, complicated dynamics underscore why Wills represent merely one component of a comprehensive estate plan.

> **Reflection:** *Would your estate go through a testate or an intestate proceeding if you passed away today?*

How Courts Determine If a Will Is Real (Valid)

Before courts can even begin to address the distribution of assets outlined in a Will, they must first determine whether the Will itself is legally valid. This threshold step is critical because an invalid Will cannot guide the probate process at all. Accordingly, the next consideration is how courts decide if a Will is genuine and enforceable.

For a Will to be valid, the law requires that certain rules be followed to ensure that the document presented as a Will is, in fact, an authentic expression of the deceased's wishes. Each state has its own specific rules that govern the verification of a Will. Such rules include:

- ⇒ The person creating the will (testator) must be at least 18 years old.
- ⇒ The Will has to be written (not verbal).
- ⇒ The testator must possess a sound mind and memory. This requirement means that when one creates the Will, one should fully understand the nature of the document, the assets he/she owns, and the consequences of their decisions.
- ⇒ The testator must sign the Will at the end.
- ⇒ The Will must be witnessed by two *disinterested* people (people who are not receiving anything from the Will).
- ⇒ Many states also require Wills to be notarized.

Generally, meeting these requirements makes a Will legally valid. Yet, even a valid Will is not beyond dispute.

Testament in Turmoil: The People Who Dare to Challenge the Will

Even though the decedent declared their wishes in the Will, this declaration does not conclude the matter. Instead, probate allows a process where an *interested* party (a person or entity with a direct legally recognized stake in the estate proceeding) can challenge the Will if he/she has been *disinherited* or if he/she disagrees with how the Will divides assets.

Wills carry a presumption of validity when they are done in accordance with the general requirements mentioned earlier. This means that Wills are assumed to be legally valid and enforceable, unless proven otherwise. Therefore, if there is a legal dispute about the Will, the burden is on the party challenging the validity to present sufficient evidence that the document is flawed or should be invalidated. An interested person displeased with the Will's instructions can challenge the Will on the grounds of:

⇒ The creator lacked capacity
⇒ Evidence of undue influence, duress, or coercion
⇒ Existence of prior Wills not properly revoked
⇒ Evidence of fraud or forgery
⇒ Improper execution

Typically, the only people who can legally challenge a Will are those who have a direct financial interest in the estate—either heirs who would have inherited if there were no Will, but were excluded, beneficiaries named in the current Will, or beneficiaries under a prior Will who were later removed. For example, if a Will does not name a child or grandchild, they may be able to argue that they were forgotten—not intentionally excluded—and may have the right to a greater portion of the estate. Estranged children are common challengers. Also, Will contests are common when the decedent had no children and extended family members litigate their claims to the estate. Will challenges are not limited to heirs or family members; friends, charities, or other entities who were named in a prior Will but omitted from a later Will may also have the legal right to contest.

Lack of Capacity

Among the most frequently raised grounds for such contests is the argument that the decedent lacked the mental capacity to execute the Will. This issue of capacity goes to the heart of whether the document can truly reflect the testator's intent. Lack of capacity in signing a Will means that the testator did not have the mental ability to understand what he or she was signing. Courts generally ask whether the person knew that he/she was making a Will, understood the property they owned, recognized their natural heirs, and understood how the Will distributed their property.

Capacity can be called into question if the testator was taking heavy medication, living with a cognitive diagnosis such as dementia or Alzheimer's, recovering from surgery, or otherwise impaired by illness, grief, or substance use. In such cases, the Will may be challenged as invalid.

To determine whether incapacity existed, courts often look at medical records, testimony from doctors or caregivers, and statements from witnesses who observed the signing. These factors do not automatically prove incapacity, but they can raise serious red flags. The court will look at the totality of the circumstances preceding the Will's creation and at the Will signing to attempt to recreate a clear picture of the testator's state of mind. Yet, even when capacity is present, a Will can be contested if it is the product of pressure or manipulation. This is where the doctrine of *undue influence* must be discussed.

Undue Influence/Duress/Coercion

A Will may be contested for undue influence if the testator was physically or mentally impaired and therefore vulnerable. The claim argues that a caretaker exploited this vulnerability to pressure the testator into signing a Will that benefited the caretaker at the expense of the testator's wishes. The linchpin of undue influence is that the testator was pressured because the wrongdoer had a close relationship with the testator, reflecting a position of power over the testator that allowed him/her to overreach and control the testator. The importance of this is that the testator is vulnerable or feeble and reliant on this wrongdoer, and so complies with the commands of the wrongdoer to avoid harm or neglect. We see this often in a caretaker relationship when a family member or friend falls ill and relies on that caretaker for care. To avoid potential suffering, the testator acquiesces to signing the Will even if it is to their family's detriment. For example, dad has been diagnosed with kidney failure, and his girlfriend influences him to change his estate plan so that all of dad's assets go to the girlfriend instead of his children. The plan is often carried out in stealth, and the family is unaware about what has been done until after the testator passes away.

In this example, undue influence is an argument that can be argued in court to undo what the bad actor attempted. Continuing with the above example, dad's children can file a petition to undo the girlfriend's actions if the court finds that the girlfriend was guilty of undue influence. To win a case based on undue influence, one must prove that 1) there was a caretaker dynamic; 2) the person was vulnerable and reliant on the caretaker; 3) the caretaker coerced the vulnerable person to change their plan; and 4) it was done in secret.

Duress is like undue influence in that the testator is compelled to act against their true wishes. However, duress typically involves threats or physical harm, whereas undue influence may rely on more subtle tactics such as manipulation, deception, or exploiting a testator's vulnerability.

Coercion, like duress, but broader as it does not always involve direct threats. Coercion can include relentless pressure, intimidation, or harassment that breaks down the testator's free will. The key element is that the testator is essentially bullied or worn down into compliance. For example, a caregiver constantly berates an elder, saying "I will abandon you unless the Will is changed," leaving the elder feeling they have "no choice."

I have seen cases where people have sought to challenge a testator's Will because of a close relationship the testator had with someone other than the child (e.g., a close relationship with a niece or nephew). Intimacy (i.e., closeness) or lack thereof is not sufficient to challenge a Will. The challenger must point to how the closeness and reliance allowed the wrongdoer to coerce or threaten the testator to sign everything over to the wrongdoer because the testator was pressured and/or afraid.

Undue influence, duress, and coercion is only one way a Will can be contested. Another common dispute arises when more than one Will exists.

What Happens If There Is a Prior Will?

If a testator leaves behind more than one Will and fails to validly revoke or cancel the earlier one, a conflict arises that requires judicial review to see which Will is valid. The court reviews both documents and determines which one to honor, focusing on whether the Will was properly signed or witnessed, whether the testator revoked the earlier version, and whether it clearly reflects the testator's intent.

William Shakespeare's *King Lear* offers a dramatic illustration of what can go wrong when a testator's intentions are not clearly or properly documented. In the play, King Lear decides to divide his kingdom among his three daughters based on their declarations of love for him. However, there is no written Will—no formal testamentary document—just a verbal promise and a division based on emotion and appearances.

Suppose, in a modern legal context, King Lear had signed a formal Will naming all three daughters as heirs but later attempted to "revoke" it by disinheriting Cordelia after her honest, but underwhelming, profession of love. Imagine he created a second document favoring Goneril and Regan but failed to properly execute it according to the legal requirements—perhaps it lacked witnesses or clear cancellation language.

In such a case, courts today would face the challenge of determining which instrument truly reflects King Lear's testamentary intent. If the second Will was not validly completed or failed to revoke the first one properly, the original Will might still govern—even if King Lear's personal feelings had changed. The tragic fallout of King Lear—betrayal, madness, and death—dramatizes the high stakes of unclear succession planning and the dangers of relying on informal changes to one's estate plan. This cautionary tale mirrors modern probate disputes where a testator's failure to formally revoke a prior Will or clarify their final intentions leads to costly litigation and family conflict.

Fraud and Forgery: The Ultimate Betrayal of Trust

Another serious ground for challenging a Will is fraud or forgery. Fraud occurs when someone tricks the testator into signing a document that the testator does not realize is a Will or misleads the testator about what the document says. Forgery, on the other hand, happens when a signature is faked or when parts of the Will are altered without the testator's knowledge. In both cases, the Will does not truly represent the testator's wishes. Courts take these claims very seriously, and evidence such as handwriting experts, testimony from witnesses, or inconsistencies in the document may be used to expose the fraud. If proven, a fraudulent or forged Will is considered invalid, the estate will be distributed under a prior valid Will or, if none exists, according to intestacy law.

Improper acts like those mentioned throughout this chapter are not the only dangers inherent in Will challenges. Even a well-intentioned mistake can make a Will invalid—especially when the testator creates the Will him/herself and without the help of an attorney. This is especially true with the rise of Do-It-Yourself (DIY) Wills, which can lead to improper execution and difficulties in interpretation.

Improper Execution of a Will

Improper execution is another common ground for contesting a Will. Every state has specific legal requirements for how a Will must be signed and witnessed, and if those rules are not followed, the document may be deemed invalid. For example, most states require the testator to sign the Will in the presence of at least two witnesses, who must also sign in each other's presence. If a witness is also a beneficiary, or if the Will lacks required signatures, notarization, or other formalities, a court can rule that the Will was not properly executed. In such cases, the Will may be rejected, and the estate may instead pass under a prior valid Will or through intestacy laws.

Do-It-Yourself (DIY) Wills

This risk of improperly executed Wills becomes even greater when individuals try to draft their own Wills without legal guidance. While DIY Wills may be better than having no Will at all, they often invite complications. Because they are written by non-lawyers and may not meet legal requirements. These documents are frequently incomplete, confusing, or include words or phrases that should not be there, leaving them open to disputes. In some cases, the testator may attempt to make inappropriate bequests, which can lead to significant complications in administering the estate.

Even more troubling, DIY Wills are especially vulnerable to the very challenges we have already discussed. They may fail to show that the testator had proper capacity, leaving the document open to attack. Because they are often written in private, they can give the appearance of undue influence by a caretaker or family member. Many do not clearly revoke prior Wills, creating conflicts between competing documents. Others lack proper witnesses, signatures, or notarization, making them easy targets for claims of fraud or forgery. Given these pitfalls, it is not surprising that disputes over DIY Wills frequently escalate into formal challenges.

Understanding how such contests unfold—and how rarely they succeed—underscores the importance of proper estate planning from the outset. Will contests are a specialized form of litigation that is extremely contentious and rarely result in the desired outcome of the challenger winning. The chances of contesting a Will and winning are slim. Research shows that only 0.5% to 3% of Wills in the United States undergo contests, with most Will contests ending up unsuccessful.[1] You will need valid grounds and evidence to contest a Will. Speculation, vengeance, jealousy, unresolved family disputes, and the pursuit of control are among the least valid grounds on which to contest a Will.

---

[1] Schoenblum, Jeffrey A. "Will Contests—An Empirical Study." *Real Property, Probate and Trust Journal*, vol. 22, 1987, pp. 607–55. An empirical study by Professor Jeffrey A. Schoenblum, published in the *Real Property, Probate and Trust Journal*, analyzed probate records in Davidson County, Tennessee, and found that approximately 0.86% of wills were contested. The *Nevada Law Journal* notes that approximately 3% of all Wills filed in the U.S. are contested

If you believe you have a solid stance to challenge a Will, you still need to consult with a lawyer and discuss how realistic your chances are. In some cases, a testator may include a no-contest clause in their final Will. This is an optional clause that some Will writers may agree to discourage contests. In such cases, you may be disinherited should your contest end in failure, leaving you with nothing from the Will. Furthermore, many probate attorneys have decided not to take on Will contest cases for the unpleasant nature of this type of litigation. It brings out the worst in people, and many probate attorneys like myself have enough experience to avoid probate litigation. Conversely, many attorneys use it as part of their business plan to make money even if success is unlikely. It is worth it to their bottom line to pursue the case even if the likelihood of success is slim. So, choose wisely if you decide to challenge a Will.

From Family Home to State Auction Block: How the State Auctions Off Your Property

Many people believe that if you die without a Will or estate plan, the state immediately takes everything you own. That is not entirely true—but the reality is not much better. If you leave no Will, your property is distributed under intestacy law, which means the court looks for your closest relatives to inherit. But here is the problem: if your family lacks the money, knowledge, or ability to probate your estate, the process stalls. The property may sit unclaimed. Creditors may come after it. The state may eventually step in to liquidate the estate to settle debts.

Even if there are no debts on the property, it does not automatically pass to your family. Without probate, the title remains frozen in your name. This means your loved ones cannot legally sell it, transfer it, or even refinance it. In the meantime, taxes, insurance, and maintenance costs continue to build. If those obligations go unpaid, the county can auction the property—even if it was once debt-free.

The process known as *escheat*, (pronounced: (uhs-CHEET) meaning *to the State*, occurs when the state permanently claims your assets or takes ownership. If no eligible relatives are found after a thorough search, the assets will eventually escheat to the state. This process ensures that no assets are left unclaimed, and it prevents assets from remaining unassigned indefinitely. Most states have a three-year deadline for unclaimed property to pass to state ownership. Once assets like real estate are transferred to the state, the state typically sells them through a public auction or similar process. The proceeds from the sale then go into the state treasury, often allocated to a specific fund or used in the state's budget. As of February 2024, New York State has reported $18.4 billion in unclaimed money and 30 million unclaimed accounts, some of which date back to the 1940s!

But make no mistake: even when heirs exist, their inability to probate can still lead to the same painful result. A family home, a car, or even cherished heirlooms can end up sold to strangers, not because you had no family, but because no plan was in place.

Takeaways

(1) Probate is the process to determine who is a rightful heir.

(2) The probate process is cumbersome and costly due to the complexities that can arise. It is prudent to meet with an experienced estate attorney to clarify how you wish to leave gifts to your loved ones.

(3) Having a Will clarifies your intentions but does not shield your family from probate because the Will still needs to be verified by the court.

(4) Although useful and better than dying intestate, a Will does not guarantee that conflicts will not arise because:

- ⇒ Wills can be challenged based on lack of capacity, undue influence, duress, coercion, fraud or forgery, or conflicting prior Wills.
- ⇒ Will contests can fracture families and rack up significant legal fees.
- ⇒ DIY Wills often fail to meet legal requirements (e.g., proper witnessing, clarity, revocation, improper execution), making them vulnerable to contests or interpretation.
- ⇒ A poorly executed Will can be as bad—or worse—than no Will at all.

(5) Even when heirs exist, their inability to probate can still lead to the same painful result of your estate remaining unclaimed and result in the state auctioning your belongings.

Chapter 2:
I Do Not Own Much—What Is the Value of a Trust for Me?

Ask Yourself... Do you believe trusts are only for wealthy families?

Based on the discussion in the previous chapter, I hope you understand that simply having a Will is insufficient, which is why trusts have become the estate planning tool that ensures a smooth transfer of assets from the decedent to heirs. Trusts are not all the same. They come in many forms, each created for a specific purpose. Choosing the right one is essential, and it is a decision best made with your attorney so that the trust aligns with your goals and protects your family's future.

At its core, a trust is a legal arrangement in which one party (called the *grantor* or *settlor*) transfers assets to another party (the *trustee*) to manage and hold for the benefit of a third party (the *beneficiary*). Trusts are not one-size-fits-all. Rather, different trusts achieve different aims depending on the needs of the client. Additionally, for a trust to work or operate properly, it must be *funded*. This means the assets—whether real estate or financial accounts—must be legally transferred into the trust. For real estate, this is done by creating a new deed that names the trust as the property owner. That deed must then be filed (or recorded) with the county where the property is located. Likewise, financial accounts fund trusts by transferring ownership from the individual's name to the trust's name. This process is called *retitling*, which means the trust becomes the official asset owner, not the individual. Both real estate and accounts can be retitled to a trust.

Let us discuss the various types of trusts and when they are ideal for certain families. This is not an exhaustive list of trusts, but those commonly used.

Revocable Living Trust

A *Revocable Living Trust,* also called a *Living Trust* or *Intervivos Trust,* is a legal document that is created by an individual called a *Grantor* or *Settlor.* A revocable trust has three major parties: the Grantor or Settlor, *Trustee*(s), and *Beneficiaries.* Grantor and Settlor are used interchangeably and mean the same thing, which is the creator of the Trust. Trustee is the person(s) charged with taking care of the Trust property or assets. Beneficiaries are those who, when the Grantor dies, receive the property. With a revocable living trust, the same person serves all three roles; the grantor is also the trustee, managing trust assets for their own benefit during their lifetime and the beneficiary. The trust's terms dictate how assets are invested, spent, or transferred—all while avoiding probate. *Revocable* means that the Grantor can change or amend the document. A Revocable Trust can hold personal property, bank accounts, annuities, brokerage accounts, or real property. Despite being placed in the trust, the Grantor is still the owner and continues to report the asset on their income tax return. Also, when the trust holds real property, the Grantor continues to control and enjoy the real property for his/her lifetime and is responsible for its maintenance and taxes as if the individual still owned the property or asset. Many individuals prefer a revocable trust because it allows flexibility to change later.

Revocable Living Trusts also provide instructions that if the Grantor becomes incapacitated and is unable to make decisions on their own, then the *Successor Trustee(s)*, come in to take care of the needs and maintenance of the Grantor. A successor trustee is a person designated to take over the management and administration of the trust after the original trustee is unable/unwilling to continue. Once the grantor dies, the Revocable Trust becomes *irrevocable*. It becomes irrevocable because it can no longer be changed or amended because the original creator has passed away.

The main goals of a revocable trust is to allow a person to privately manage their assets during their lifetime and ensure a smooth, private transfer of those assets after death—without going through probate. In dealing with financial accounts, when the grantor dies, the successor trustee simply shows the bank/brokerage proof of their authority (trust document or certificate of trust, plus a death certificate). The financial institution then changes control of the account from the grantor/trustee to the successor trustee. The successor trustee distributes the funds according to the trust's instructions (writes checks, transfers funds, or opens new accounts for beneficiaries).

In terms of real estate, a revocable trust allows for the smooth transfer of title from the trust to the future beneficiary. This is usually done by preparing and recording a new deed with the county recorder that changes ownership from the trust to the beneficiary, when the grantor dies. The most common deed used for this is a Trustee's Deed or Executor's Deed (depending on the situation). The deed shows the transfer from the trustee (acting under the authority of the trust) to the named beneficiary. This is how probate is avoided. Do you see how trust simplifies inheriting assets upon death and how much more robust protection is offered when compared to a Will?

Irrevocable Trusts

Like revocable trusts, irrevocable trusts are effective tools for avoiding probate and can provide for the easy transfer of assets at death. Both involve the same key parties: a grantor, trustee, successor trustee, and beneficiaries. The key difference is that, once established, an irrevocable trust generally cannot be changed, modified, or revoked by the grantor. This permanence is what gives it its name. In addition, once assets are transferred into an irrevocable trust, the grantor usually gives up ownership and control of those assets permanently, which can provide tax and asset protection benefits. Here are some key aspects of irrevocable trusts:

> (1) **Permanent and Unchangeable**: Once created, an irrevocable trust <u>cannot be changed, amended, or revoked</u> by the grantor, except in rare cases with the permission of beneficiaries or by court order.

(2) **Medicaid Long-Term Care Eligibility**: Irrevocable trusts are often used for Medicaid Long-Term Care planning to protect assets from being counted in eligibility determinations.

    a. Also, protects disabled beneficiaries from losing needs-based federal and state benefits such as Social Security Insurance, Medicaid, SNAP, TANF, and housing assistance.

(3) **Estate Taxes:** Because assets in an irrevocable trust are removed from the grantor's estate, they are typically not subject to estate taxes upon the grantor's death. This makes irrevocable trusts an effective tool for reducing estate taxes, particularly for high-net-worth individuals.

(4) **No Personal Ownership of Assets**: The grantor relinquishes control and ownership of the assets placed into the trust.

(5) **Asset Protection:** Shields assets from creditors, lawsuits, or divorces.

To achieve these objectives, a properly written irrevocable trust includes specific language that the United States Internal Revenue Service (IRS) requires for special tax benefits and that Medicaid Long-Term Care uses to determine eligibility. This language lets the IRS and Medicaid Long-Term Care know how to treat the trust and its assets. Without the correct language, the trust might not qualify for these benefits, potentially causing tax issues or Medicaid Long-Term Care ineligibility. Below are some examples of important Medicaid Long-Term Care and IRS language to watch for:

(1) Irrevocability Clause

⇒ The trust must explicitly state that it is irrevocable.

⇒ Example: *"This trust is irrevocable and shall not be subject to amendment, modification, or revocation by the Grantor or any other party."*

(2) No Access to Principal for the Grantor:

⇒ There must be language that states that the creator of the trust cannot take back any of the money or property placed into the trust. Once the assets are in the trust, they are no longer the grantor's property.

⇒ Example: *"The Grantor shall have no right to receive distributions of principal from this trust. The trustee shall not have discretion to distribute trust principal to the Grantor under any circumstances."*

(3) Spendthrift Clause

⇒ This clause protects the trust assets from the creditors of the beneficiaries, ensuring that trust assets are only available to the beneficiaries under the terms of the trust.

⇒ Example: *"No interest of any beneficiary in the income or principal of this trust shall be subject to voluntary or involuntary transfer, sale, assignment, pledge, or alienation, nor shall it be subject to claims of creditors or others."*

(4) No Reversionary Interests Clause

⇒ The grantor should not retain any rights to benefit from the trust, such as receiving income or reclaiming the assets after transferring them into the trust. This ensures the assets are truly out of the grantor's estate.

⇒ Example: *"The Grantor shall have no reversionary interests or power to reclaim the trust assets at any time."*

(5) Explicit Purpose for Medicaid Long-Term Care Planning:

⇒ The trust can be specifically designed to protect the Grantor's assets from being counted as resources when applying for Medicaid Long-Term Care or other government benefits that require financial eligibility tests.

⇒ Example: *"This trust is created for the primary purpose of preserving assets while maintaining the Grantor's eligibility for Medicaid Long-Term Care and other means-tested benefits. It is the intention of the Grantor that all provisions be construed to achieve this purpose."*

(6) Power to Substitute Assets

⇒ This power allows the Grantor to swap assets within the Trust for assets of equivalent value. This power is often used for tax planning, allowing the Grantor to retain certain tax attributes while still treating the trust as an Irrevocable Trust.

⇒ Example: *The Grantor reserves the power to substitute assets of equivalent value, solely for tax purposes, without impacting the trust's irrevocable status."*

These clauses help clarify the grantor's limited rights and intent, supporting the desired public benefit eligibility, such as Medicaid Long-Term Care and/or IRS treatment.

How Much Power Are You Giving Up?

The concept of surrendering one's assets to an irrevocable trust can be unsettling. However, the grantor retains limited powers for tax or lifestyle purposes, but gives up legal ownership (the trust now owns the asset). Transferring ownership of the assets is a key requirement for a trust to be considered irrevocable. However, the powers the grantor relinquishes are balanced by meaningful control retained at the outset. For example, the grantor selects the trustee—a person or institution they trust to carry out their wishes faithfully—and designs the structure of the trust itself. This includes naming the beneficiaries, defining the specific terms and conditions under which assets will be distributed, and determining whether distributions will be made outright, in stages, or subject to certain life events or milestones. In this way, the grantor still shapes the legacy they are leaving behind. Even though day-to-day control and legal ownership are surrendered, the trust reflects the grantor's values, priorities, and intentions. It allows them to protect their loved ones, provide financial stability across generations, and preserve assets in a way that a simple Will cannot. So, while irrevocable trusts require letting go of certain powers, they also empower the grantor to craft a detailed and lasting plan that carries out their wishes long after they are gone.

> **Reflection:** *Could a trust simplify things for your family?*

There Is No Place Like Home

For many families, the home is far more than simply an asset—it is a place of stability, identity, and emotional security. Shelter is a basic human need, and in the United States, homeownership remains one of the most significant ways individuals build and preserve wealth across generations. Ensuring that this asset is properly protected and passed on is not only a financial decision but a deeply personal one rooted in the desire to safeguard loved ones from uncertainty or displacement. By placing a home into a trust, individuals take a proactive step toward securing their family's future. Firstly, it helps prevent the risk of the property becoming entangled in the probate process, as discussed earlier. Additionally, it ensures that family members—especially children or vulnerable relatives—are not left without shelter or forced to sell the home under distress. In this way, transferring real estate into a trust is about more than preserving value; it is about preserving the sense of safety, continuity, and belonging that a home represents.

While there are many different types of irrevocable trusts, this section will focus specifically on three (3) that are most relevant for practical estate planning:

⇒ Special Needs Trusts (SNTs)
⇒ Simple Trusts
⇒ Irrevocable Trusts for Medicaid Long-Term Care Eligibility (discussed in the next chapter)

Caring for Your Vulnerable Children with Trusts

In the same way that transferring real estate into a trust can preserve stability for a family, certain trusts can also be designed to protect vulnerable children and secure their care while maintaining eligibility for public benefits. If you have children who are disabled and they rely on state benefits for care, then you also must consider a Special Needs Trust (SNT). Special Needs Trust, Supplemental Needs Trusts, or SNTs, are a special type of irrevocable trust designed for people with disabilities. Under federal statute and many states' laws, SNTs allow a trustee to manage funds for the benefit of a person with a disability while preserving that person's eligibility for government benefits. The funds set aside in an SNT support a person with a severe and chronic disability—both now and in the future, when the creator of the trust may no longer be there to oversee their care. An SNT is designed to cover the beneficiary's unique, long-term needs and to provide the best possible quality of life. At the same time, it avoids giving the disabled person so much money that he/she loses eligibility for essential government programs such as Basic Medicaid, Social Security Disability, or Medicaid Long-Term Care.

These trusts operate by supplementing rather than replacing these benefits, covering expenses that enhance the beneficiary's quality of life (e.g., medical expenses, therapies, personal care, and recreational activities) without disqualifying the beneficiary from necessary support. Any person may create an SNT for the benefit of any disabled person, whether related to him/her or not. The most common creators of SNTs are parents of disabled children, but they can be created by anyone, such as a grandparent, or other relative, or sympathetic person.

An SNT is a must to have in place so that your child can continue to have a comfortable life in the event you are not there to care for them. The likelihood of your children outliving you is also another reason why an SNT is a necessity. There are two primary types of SNTs:

⇒ **First-Party SNTs**: Funded with the disabled individual's own assets, often funded from money won in a legal settlement or inheritance. These must comply with Medicaid (may include Medicaid Long-Term Care) payback rules, meaning any remaining funds in the trust at the beneficiary's death may be subject to Medicaid reimbursement.

⇒ **Third-Party SNTs**: Established and funded by someone other than the disabled individual, typically a parent or grandparent. These funds are not subject to Medicaid Long-Term Care payback and can pass to other beneficiaries upon the death of the disabled person.

Placing Financial Accounts into An Irrevocable Trust

Special Needs Trusts are designed to protect disabled beneficiaries, but not every family needs this type of planning. For others, a different irrevocable trust—one focused on steady income rather than government benefits—may be a better fit. So, another type of irrevocable trust is a *simple trust,* which is typically designed to distribute all its income to beneficiaries each year, without distributing the *principal.* The principal (the original money or property placed into the trust) is preserved and not distributed.

Simple trusts are useful for families who want to create a steady stream of income for loved ones, while ensuring that the underlying assets remain intact for the future. Families who may chose a Simple Irrevocable Trust include:

⇒ **Families who want a steady income for their heirs**. For example, parents who want their adult children to receive regular financial support from investments, but also want to make sure the core assets remain intact for later inheritance.

⇒ **Surviving Spouses**: A simple trust can provide annual income for a surviving husband or wife, while preserving the principal for children or grandchildren after that spouse passes.

⇒ **Families with modest estates that want an uncomplicated trust**: Unlike more complex trusts used for tax shelters or Medicaid planning, a simple trust works well for families who want a no-frills way to pass on income without the risks of overspending or mismanagement.

All of this may sound technical, but the idea is simple. Let us bring it to life with a story.

Goldie And the Magic Orchard – A Trust Income Tale

Once upon a time, in a peaceful kingdom, there lived a kind queen named Goldie. As she grew older, she wanted to make sure her children—Ella and Max—were taken care of, even after she was gone.

So, Goldie went to the royal wizard (her estate planner) and created a magical chest called an Irrevocable Trust. Into this chest, she placed:

⇒ *A golden apple orchard that produced fruit every year*
⇒ *A goose that laid golden eggs once a month*
⇒ *A pouch of treasure that earned interest in the royal bank*

The trust was overseen by a loyal knight named Sir Trustee, who followed Goldie's instructions to the letter. Each year, the orchard produced bushels of apples, the goose laid golden eggs, and the treasure pouch from the bank's magic grew from interest. These were all income—money or goods the trust earned without touching the original gifts.

Sir Trustee gathered this income and delivered it to Ella and Max as their allowance, just like the queen wished. Though the magical chest still held the orchard, the goose, and the pouch (the principal), only the income—the apples, eggs, and interest—was given out to Ella and Max.

And so, Ella and Max lived happily ever after with their yearly gift of apples, golden eggs, and growing treasure, thanks to the power of trust income.

Hopefully, this illustration helps clarify how trust income works: the principal is preserved, while the earnings provide steady support for loved ones.

Trusts Pay a Lot in Taxes, So Strategic Planning Matters

While Goldie's story makes trust income sound simple, the reality is more complex for trust taxes. Trusts do not just provide income to beneficiaries—they also create tax responsibilities, and those can be significant if not carefully planned. Understanding who is responsible for paying the tax—the trust, the beneficiary, or the grantor—can significantly impact the total amount of tax owed.

As a reminder, these tax rules apply solely to irrevocable trusts, since revocable trusts remain part of the grantor's estate and are taxed directly to the grantor. Because irrevocable trusts are subject to higher tax rates at much lower income limits than individuals, careful planning is essential. Unlike individual taxpayers, who do not reach the top federal income tax rate of 37 percent until they earn over $600,000, trusts hit that same rate with just $14,451 of taxable income.[2] In 2025, the tax brackets for trusts remain steep: income over $3,150 is already taxed at 24 percent, and trust income over $11,500 jumps to 35 percent. Due to this steep tax structure, it is often more tax-efficient to distribute trust income to beneficiaries, who are taxed at more favorable individual rates. Then, the trust deducts these distributions, and the beneficiaries report these distributions they receive as income on their tax returns.

Smart trust planning can significantly reduce the overall tax burden by designing a trust that permit the individual beneficiaries to pay taxes on distributions rather than the trust. See this chart to compare income tax rates for individuals compared to trust income.

---

[2] United States, Internal Revenue Service. Form 1041-ES: Estimated Income Tax for Estates and Trusts. Department of the Treasury, 2025. https://www.irs.gov/pub/irs-pdf/f1041es.pdf.

2025 Federal Income Tax Brackets Comparison

Taxable Income	Trusts & Estates	Single Individuals
$0 – $3,150	10%	10%: $0 – $11,925
$3,151 – $11,450	24%	12%: $11,926 – $48,475
$11,451 – $15,650	35%	22%: $48,476 – $103,350
$15,651+	37%	37%: $626,351+

Takeaways:

(1) There are different types of trusts based on the client's needs. Revocable Trusts and Irrevocable Trusts differ in their objective, but both are probate avoidant tools and can be useful even if a person has modest assets.

(2) Specific conditions must be in the irrevocable trust for Medicaid and other needs-based government program eligibility.

(3) Assets need to fund a trust: If a trust is not properly funded, it may not control or protect the assets as intended.

(4) Trusts are taxed at much higher rates than individuals.

(5) Effective trust planning often involves distributing income to beneficiaries or using trust structures that shift the tax burden away from the trust itself. Because individual beneficiaries

typically face lower income tax rates than trusts, this strategy can reduce overall taxes on trust earnings.

Key Differences Between Revocable and Irrevocable Trust

Feature	Revocable Trust	Irrevocable Trust
Control	Grantor retains full control; can modify or revoke at any time	Grantor relinquishes control and cannot modify or revoke; control passes to trustee
Ownership / Legal Title	Grantor is considered the owner	Trust owns the assets; the grantor gives up ownership
Tax Treatment	Income taxed on grantor's personal return; assets included in estate	Trust usually taxed separately; assets generally excluded from grantor's estate
Asset Protection	No protection from creditors or lawsuits	Strong protection from creditors, lawsuits, and divorce claims
Medicaid / Government Benefits	Assets count toward eligibility	Properly structured, assets do **not** count; may trigger look-back penalty if recently transferred

Privacy	Avoids probate; assets private upon death	Avoids probate; assets separate from grantor's estate
Typical Uses	Avoid probate, simplify estate transfer, maintain flexibility	Asset protection, tax planning, charitable giving, Medicaid planning, controlling asset use after death

Chapter 3:
How Irrevocable Trusts Impact Medicaid Long-Term Care Eligibility

Ask Yourself... Did you know that without proper planning, Medicaid can place a lien on your assets to recoup the cost of your Medicaid Long-Term care costs?

As mentioned in the previous chapter, if you are concerned about long-term medical care costs and wish to become Medicaid Long-Term Care eligible, then an Irrevocable Trust may be the appropriate planning tool for you. Due to the extraordinarily high cost of home care and nursing home care—sometimes priced at $10,000 or more per month—few can afford to cover their long-term care and so rely on Medicaid Long-Term Care to cover the cost. Currently, more than 1.3 million Americans live in nursing homes, paid for through Medicaid Long-Term Care.[3] However, getting approved for Medicaid Long-Term Care can be tricky.

Many seniors rely on Medicare, a federal health insurance program that primarily serves individuals aged 65 and older (along with certain younger people with disabilities). Medicare does **not** cover most long-term care services and only covers some medical care for 100 days. Medicaid, on the other hand, includes a separate program—Medicaid Long-Term Care—

---

[3] **Centers for Disease Control and Prevention.** "Nursing Home Care." *FastStats*, National Center for Health Statistics, 24 May 2023, www.cdc.gov/nchs/fastats/nursing-home-care.htm. Accessed 23 Sept. 2025.

designed specifically to help eligible seniors pay for extended care such as nursing homes or in-home assistance. This distinction is important: standard Medicaid covers general medical needs for low-income individuals, while Medicaid Long-Term Care addresses the ongoing and often high-cost support services needed by aging adults. Medicaid Long-Term Care is a government-funded health insurance program that helps older adults or certain disabled adults—usually age 65 and older—pay for long-term care services that Medicare does not cover. This includes two major types of support:

⇒ **Nursing Home Care:** Full-time residential care in a licensed facility, including medical supervision, personal care, meals, and room and board.

⇒ **Home and Community-Based Services (HCBS):** In-home support for seniors who wish to remain in their own homes. Services can include help with bathing, dressing, meal preparation, medication management, and sometimes skilled nursing.

For seniors in nursing homes, Medicaid Long-Term Care usually pays a set daily rate that covers the resident's room and board, nursing care, and any necessary medical supplies or services, therapy, and social activities. However, some personal items or services, like private rooms or special amenities, may not be covered and may require additional out-of-pocket payments. Home and Community-Based Services, or Home Care programs, are designed to help eligible elderly or disabled individuals remain safely at home, rather than in a nursing home. So, instead of an elderly person going into nursing home facilities, Home Care programs allow an individual to have a Home Attendant who assists with housekeeping services such as cleaning, cooking, bathing, and grooming.

Home Care services are gaining momentum throughout the country as an alternative to nursing homes because of the nursing home crisis. The shortage of "beds," staffing shortages, and a decrease in new construction of facilities render many nursing home facilities without the capacity to admit new Medicaid Long-Term Care residents. In addition, new facility construction has slowed because it depends on Medicaid Long-Term Care reimbursement, which is typically low. Meanwhile, the cost of building exceeds the rising costs of construction and financing, making development financially unsustainable[4], according to the American Health Care Association (AHCA). From 2020 to the present, 579 nursing homes have closed, and more than 21,000 residents have been displaced by closures. Moreover, 30 additional counties have become what AHCA calls *nursing home*

---

[4]American Health Care Association and National Center for Assisted Living. Access Report: Closing the Gap in Nursing Home Care. AHCA/NCAL, 2024.https://www.ahcancal.org/News-and-Communications/Fact-Sheets/Access-Report-2024.pdf.

deserts.[5] That means 45, 217 fewer nursing home beds were available to prospective residents due to downsizing.[6]

Both Nursing Home Medicaid and HCBS follow similar financial eligibility rules, but HCBS usually has more restrictions because of limited spots. For both programs, you must show a medical need for long-term care.

Medicaid Long-Term Care Eligibility

Medicaid Long-Term Care eligibility is based on income and assets. This means if someone has too many assets or too much income, they may be disqualified from receiving Medicaid Long-Term Care. Therefore, if someone intends to rely on Medicaid Long-Term Care, then it is prudent to begin transferring their assets out of their name. Transferring assets from their name and into an irrevocable trust, as discussed earlier, and *spending down* is how many qualify for Medicaid Long-Term Care. Spending down refers to the process of reducing countable income or assets to meet Medicaid's strict financial limits. An applicant must reduce both their income and assets to qualify.

---

[5] Geographic areas—often rural or underserved urban communities—where access to nursing homes is severely limited or non-existent. These areas lack enough facilities to meet the long-term care needs of the aging population.

[6] Stulick, Amy. "Nearly 450K Residents at Risk of Displacement if Mandate Is Enacted, As Access Issues Compound." *Skilled Nursing News*, 23 Aug. 2023, skillednursingnews.com/2023/08/nearly-450k-residents-at-risk-of-displacement-if-mandate-is-enacted-as-access-issues-compound/.

Because Medicaid is a needs-based program, applicants must have limited resources to qualify. Medicaid treats income as something that "comes in" each month (like Social Security, pensions, or wages). To qualify for that month, an applicant's income must fall under the Medicaid limit after subtracting allowable medical expenses. If your countable income is too high, you must show you have applied the "excess" income to medical bills for that month. The next month, the process starts over again when one receives new income. Here is typically how the spend down works: If your income is above the Medicaid limit in your state, you may still qualify by applying excess income toward medical expenses. This can include:

⇒ Nursing home bills
⇒ Doctor visits and hospital costs
⇒ Prescription drugs
⇒ Medically necessary supplies
⇒ Health insurance premiums, co-pays, deductibles

When your medical expenses lower your income below the Medicaid eligibility threshold, you qualify for Medicaid for that month. In most states, income spend down is a month-by-month process, not a yearly one.

You may be wondering whether you can count your living expenses, like mortgage payments, rent, utilities, internet, and food, toward reducing your income. Generally, these living expenses are excluded unless they are directly tied to a medical need, such as room and board in a licensed assisted living or nursing home.

Medicaid also limits the amount of countable assets you can own (for example, $2,000 in your bank account for most states for a single person). To qualify, people spend down their resources by using excess savings on:

⇒ Paying off debts
⇒ Prepaying funeral and burial expenses (through Medicaid-compliant burial funds)
⇒ Making necessary home repairs or modifications
⇒ Purchasing exempt items like medical equipment, clothing, or personal needs

Importantly, you cannot simply give assets away — Medicaid has a *look-back period* (usually 5 years) to prevent people from transferring assets below market value to qualify sooner. Transfers made during the Medicaid application period can result in a penalty period during which Medicaid will not pay for care. We will discuss the look-back period later in this chapter.

What Income and Assets Count to Determine Medicaid Long-Term Care Eligibility?

The federal government establishes basic parameters for the Medicaid Long-Term Care eligibility, yet each state sets its own rules within these parameters. This means all 50 states have varying Medicaid Long-Term Care eligibility programs, and states do not share universal rules. Again, income is money that comes in regularly, whether monthly or occasionally. Medicaid looks at it on a month-to-month basis. Nearly all sources of income are counted toward Medicaid Long-Term Care's income limit. This includes employment wages, alimony payments, pensions, Social Security Disability Income, Social Security Income, gifts, annuity payments, and IRA distributions. Nationally, Holocaust restitution payments are not counted as income. Additionally, *VA Aid and Attendance Benefits and Housebound Allowance*—which is beyond the Basic VA Pension—does not count as income.[7]

In many cases, Medicaid Long-Term Care requires recipients to contribute most of their monthly income toward their cost of care. This is known as the *patient pay amount* or *share of cost*. Medicaid Long-Term Care then covers the remaining balance, ensuring that the person's basic needs are met while still receiving care.

As income is based on regular, recurring payments, assets are things you already own that could be used or spent down to pay for your care. Countable assets calculated toward Medicaid Long-Term Care's asset limit include: cash, stocks, bonds, investments, vacation homes, and bank accounts (i.e., checking, savings, money market). There are also exempt (non-countable)

---

[7]Medicaid Long-Term Care Planning Assistance. "Medicaid Long-Term Care Eligibility—New York." *Medicaid Long-Term CarePlanningAssistance.org*, 3 Mar. 2025, www.Medicaid Long-Term Careplanningassistance.org/Medicaid Long-Term Care-eligibility-new-york/.

assets. An asset is considered exempt, or non-countable, when a person can legally keep it or not have to spend it down and still qualify for Medicaid Long-Term Care.[8] Exemptions generally include one's primary home, personal belongings, household items, a vehicle, burial funds up to $1,500, or a life insurance policy with a cash value up to $1,500, and non-refundable prepaid funeral agreements. In some states, IRAs and 401(k) plans in payout status, meaning that the person is receiving the minimum required distributions, are exempt. Alternatively, in some states, IRAs and 401(k)s in payout status are countable assets.

Does Medicaid Long-Term Care Count My Spouse's Income?

When only one spouse of a married couple applies for Medicaid Long-Term Care, the non-applicant spouse's income is disregarded. Furthermore, if the non-applicant spouse relies on the income of the other spouse entering a nursing home, the state will reserve a portion of the applicant spouse's income to prevent spousal impoverishment.[9]

---

[8] Although an asset may be exempt to qualify for Medicaid Long-Term Care, it may still be subject to a Medicaid lien or Estate Recovery.

[9] Spousal Impoverishment Protections." *Medicaid Long-Term CarePlanningAssistance.org*, 4 June 2025, www.Medicaid Long-Term Careplanningassistance.org/spousal-protections/. To prevent the non-applicant spouse from becoming financially vulnerable—a situation known as "spousal impoverishment"—Medicaid Long-Term Care provides protections:
⇒ Minimum Monthly Maintenance Needs Allowance (MMMNA): This is the minimum amount of monthly income the non-applicant spouse is entitled to

When only one spouse applies for Medicaid Long-Term Care (called the *institutionalized spouse*, the non-applicant spouse, known as the *community spouse*), may be able to retain a higher amount of assets. This is referred to as the *Community Spouse Resource Allowance* (CSRA), up to the maximum of $148,620 (2024 federal guideline). These rules prevent the community spouse from becoming impoverished while their partner receives long-term care through Medicaid. This means the community spouse can keep up to $148,620 in countable assets, while the institutionalized spouse must reduce their share to the Medicaid limit (often $2,000). For example, if a couple has $100,000 in countable assets, the institutionalized spouse must spend down to the $2,000 Medicaid asset limit. The community spouse can keep $100,000 as their CSRA because this is below the CSRA. Alternatively, if the couple has $300,000, the community spouse can only keep up to $148,620—not half—because of the federal cap.

Exempt Assets: Some common exempt or non-countable assets include:

(1) Primary residence: If it is occupied by the Medicaid Long-Term Care applicant or their spouse, it is generally exempt.

---

retain. If the non-applicant spouse's income is below this threshold, the applicant spouse can transfer a portion of their income to the non-applicant spouse to bring their income up to the MMMNA level. Medicaid Long-Term Care Planning Assistance+1Medicaid Long-Term Care Planning Assistance+1

⇒ Community Spouse Resource Allowance (CSRA): This is the portion of the couple's combined assets that the non-applicant spouse is allowed to retain. The CSRA is determined based on federal guidelines and varies by state.

Some states impose an equity limit between $730,000 and $1,097,000

(2) Personal belongings and household items

(3) One vehicle (if it is used for the applicant's or their spouse's transportation)

(4) Prepaid funeral and burial expenses

(5) Life insurance (with a cash value of typically less than $1,500)

(6) Retirement accounts (in certain states, if they are in payout status)

The primary home can be exempt from Medicaid Long-Term Care asset limits under certain conditions because Medicaid Long-Term Care recognizes it as a necessity, especially for individuals who are applying for long-term care coverage but still want to ensure their spouse or family members have a place to live. Here is how the exemption generally works:

(1) Applicant's Residence:

⇒ **Applicant Lives in the Home:** If the Medicaid Long-Term Care applicant lives in the home or intends to return to the home (even if temporarily in a nursing home or medical facility), the home is considered an exempt asset.

⇒ **Equity Limit:** There is an equity value limit for the home in many states. As of 2025, the federal Medicaid Long-Term Care guidelines set the maximum home equity limit between $730,000 and $1,097,000, depending on the state. Homes with equity above this limit might not qualify for the exemption.

(2) Spouse Living in the Home
⇒ **Community Spouse**: If the Medicaid Long-Term Care applicant is married and their spouse continues to live in the home, the home remains exempt regardless of the equity value. This protects the spouse from losing the home if the other spouse requires long-term care.

(3) Dependent Relative Living in the Home
⇒ If a dependent relative lives in the home, such as a child under 21 years of age, a blind or disabled adult child, or other dependents (like a sibling), the home remains exempt.

(4) Intention to Return Home
⇒ Even if the Medicaid Long-Term Care applicant is receiving long-term care outside of the home, if the applicant declares an intention to return home, Medicaid Long-Term Care may consider the home exempt. This is true even if it is uncertain whether the person will realistically return.

Look-Back Period

While the home may be exempt under certain conditions, Medicaid also examines past financial activity before granting coverage. This is known as the *look-back period,* during which Medicaid will review financial transactions, assets currently owned, and transferred in the previous sixty (60) months or five (5) years. The look-back period requires applicants to submit all financial information and transactions they have made within the sixty-months (60) immediately preceding their application date. These financial transactions include gifts or asset transfers for money, real property, financial assets, or other valuable items. The look-back rule's purpose is to ensure that applicants are not hiding their assets to receive Medicaid Long-Term Care benefits for which a person would not otherwise be eligible. If transfers have occurred for less than the fair market value during that period, a penalty is assessed for a period during which the applicant cannot receive benefits, or the individual may be deemed to be ineligible.

The look-back period for Medicaid Long-Term Care eligibility begins on the date of application, when the applicant is admitted into the nursing home or needs nursing home/chronic care. For example, if an individual applies for Medicaid Long-Term Care benefits on May 31, 2023, their look-back period would begin on May 1, 2018. To maximize your financial security during this crucial life stage, it is wise to begin planning as soon as possible—ideally, at least five years before reaching age 65 or needing long-term care services, to ensure that all transfers meet the applicable guidelines.

California currently has a more lenient 30-month (2.5-year) look-back period for Medicaid Long-Term Care eligibility. However, this look-back period is being phased out, and by July 2026, the look-back period for new applicants will be eliminated. Importantly, California's look-back period applies only to Nursing Home Medicaid (institutional care)—not to Home and Community-Based Services. This means that individuals applying for in-home long-term care through Medi-Cal, can transfer assets without triggering a penalty, even during the current transition period.

The Medicaid Long-Term Care Penalty Calculation Made Simple

The Medicaid Long-Term care penalty is applied when someone has transferred assets **for less than fair market value** (FMV) during Medicaid's 60-month look-back period. Please note this distinction: Medicaid Long-Term Care does not penalize transfers made for FMV; only those made for less than FMV during the look-back period. The penalty period is the amount of time Medicaid will **not** pay for the applicant's care, and it is calculated using the following formula:

Penalty Period (in months) = Total Value of Assets Transferred for Less than FMV ÷ State's Average Monthly Nursing Home Care Costs

To calculate this, you first add up the total value of all gifts, sales, or transfers made below fair market value during the look-back period. Next, you divide this amount by your state's *penalty divisor*, which is the state's average monthly cost of private-pay nursing home care. For example, in 2025, Pennsylvania's divisor is approximately $12,000, and $7,339 for Texas. Expensive, right! So, if you gave away $50,000 and your state's divisor is $10,000, the penalty would be five months, meaning Medicaid would not cover your long-term care costs for that period. Importantly, the penalty does not begin when you make the gift; it only starts when you apply for long-term care.

Some asset transfers are exempt from penalties, such as

(1) Transfers made to a spouse,
(2) Transfers made to a blind or disabled child, regardless of age, a child under 21, or
(3) Transfers to a "caregiver child" who lived with you for at least two years preceding your Medicaid Long-Term Care application, and because of their care, delayed your nursing home placement,
(4) Transfers to a sibling with an equity interest in the home (if they lived there for at least one year before your nursing home placement).

Asset transfers under these conditions and certain trust transfers, such as those into special needs trusts, are also exempt. So, even though these transfers are technically below FMV, Medicaid does not impose a penalty because the law specifically exempts them. Exempt transfer rules apply to both, the primary home and other assets, but the home is treated with special care because it is usually the largest asset most people own. The following table illustrates how exempts assets are treated.

Exempt Transfers Under Medicaid Look-Back Rules

Type of Transfer	Home (Primary Residence)	Other Assets (Cash, Investments, etc.)
To spouse	✅ Exempt	✅ Exempt
To child under 21	✅ Exempt	✅ Exempt
To blind or disabled child (any age)	✅ Exempt	✅ Exempt
To caregiver child (lived in the home ≥2 years before institutionalization and provided care that delayed nursing home placement)	✅ Exempt	❌ Not exempt
To sibling with equity interest (lived in the home ≥1 year before institutionalization)	✅ Exempt	❌ Not exempt
To a trust for the sole benefit of a disabled person	❌ Not applicable	✅ Exempt
Any other gift/transfer for less than FMV	❌ Penalty applies	❌ Penalty applies

An asset transferred for fair market value (FMV) does not trigger a Medicaid long-term care penalty, because Medicaid views it as a legitimate sale. However, the applicant must be able to prove that the transfer was for FMV. This usually means documentation such as contracts, an appraisal, a bill of sale, or other records showing that the transaction reflected the true value of the asset. Medicaid also requires evidence that the proceeds were received and accounted for (typically deposited into a bank account). Without proof, Medicaid may presume the transfer was for less than FMV and impose a penalty. Medicaid does not simply take your word that the sale was for FMV. If there is no record of the money being deposited, Medicaid may suspect the transaction was not legitimate or that the money was gifted or hidden. In such cases, Medicaid can then reclassify the transaction as a "transfer for less than FMV" and impose a penalty. If the money was not deposited into a bank, you should reconstruct the record as best you can — e.g., notes of cash received, witnesses, or receipts for how it was spent legitimately. Spending cash without documentation is risky because Medicaid may treat it as a disqualifying transfer.

Also, once you sell an asset for FMV, the cash proceeds count as an asset for Medicaid purposes. These proceeds must be spent down to meet Medicaid's asset limits, as discussed earlier.

Medicaid Long-Term Care Estate Recovery Program

While the primary home can be exempt during the applicant's lifetime to make a person Medicaid Long-Term Care eligible, Medicaid may still seek to recover long-term care costs from the home after the individual's death through the Medicaid Long-Term Care Estate Recovery Program (MERP). MERP is a program that allows states to seek reimbursement for long-term care costs. All states have a MERP, but laws governing a state's MERP vary. Some states will not attempt recovery if the deceased's estate is under a specified value.

For example, Georgia will not seek recovery if one's estate is less than $25,000, and in Texas, recovery will not be sought on an estate valued at less than $10,000. Some states may also waive Estate Recovery if the cost of Medicaid Long-Term Care is under a specific amount. While Medicaid Long-Term Care cannot attempt Estate Recovery if there is a surviving spouse, some states will attempt to collect after the death of the surviving spouse, while other states will not. California and Texas are two states that prohibit Estate Recovery until after the death of the non-Medicaid Long-Term Care spouse. Furthermore, some states only seek Estate Recovery through assets that go through probate, while other states seek reimbursement through assets that do not go through probate.

Estate Recovery is governed by the laws that are in effect at the time of a Medicaid Long-Term Care recipient's death, not the laws that were in place when the person became eligible for or began receiving Medicaid Long-Term Care.

> **Reflection:** *Given your current situation, could the cost of long-term care deplete your savings or result in your family having to repay a medical lien on your home?*

Takeaways:

(1) General Medicaid is different from Medicaid Long-Term Care.

(2) Medicaid Long-Term Care covers nursing home care and home and community-based services.

(3) Medicaid Long-Term Care eligibility is based on the amount of income and assets that the applicant has at the time of application.

(4) Medicaid can exempt certain assets that allow a person to be Medicaid eligible. However, Medicaid may place a lien on those assets to recoup Medicaid Long-term Care costs.

(5) Through MERP, Medicaid **may** attempt to recoup long-term care expenses once the applicant (and possibly the surviving spouse) has passed away.

(6) Spend down programs and a properly worded irrevocable trust is how many people prepare for Medicaid Long-Term Care eligibility and other needs-based programs.

(7) Medicaid Long-Term Care penalties are assessed only for assets transferred for less than FMV.

(8) There are certain assets transferred to certain family members that are exempt from penalties even though they may be transferred for less than FMV.

(9) Most states have a 60-month look-back period to review financial transactions to ensure an applicant is not hiding assets.

(10) Asset transfers for FMV are safe and do not create a penalty, but Medicaid will require documentation of the transfers and will examine how you handled the cash proceeds. Proper planning is important to avoid inadvertently triggering a penalty.

Chapter 4:
Plan for the Dreams You Chase and the Storms You Cannot See

Planning for assets matters, but planning for children matters most. To see why, step into the story of one family and the treasure they left behind.

The Treasure They Left Behind

Once upon a time, in a cozy home filled with giggles and crayon-drawn dreams, there lived a devoted couple who loved each other deeply and adored their two little daughters more than anything in the world. For years, they whispered about a magical place called Bali—a faraway land of golden sunrises, turquoise seas, and serene temples nestled among emerald hills.

They dreamed of this journey not as a fleeting escape, but as the crown jewel of their shared dreams. Every night, after bedtime stories were read and sleepy kisses planted on soft foreheads, they would sit by the fire and add to their vision board: shimmering ocean views, strolls together under starlit skies, and a stay at the legendary Aman Palace—an oasis of peace fit for royalty.

And then, one fateful spring, the dream came true.

With joyous hearts and careful planning, they arranged for their daughters to stay with their beloved grandparents—wise, warm, and full of love. Bags were packed, hugs were tight, and with the rising sun, the couple set off on their fairytale adventure.

In Bali, everything was as magical as they had imagined. The days were sundrenched and lazy, the nights soft with lantern light and laughter. Still, their thoughts never strayed far from home. They called each day, listening to the girls' stories, reminding them to brush their teeth, eat veggies, and always be kind. At night, they read bedtime tales over the phone, their voices a familiar lullaby across the miles.

But then, as if a dark spell had been cast, the tale took a cruel and sudden turn.

In the blink of an eye, under a sky still glowing with tropical sun, a tragic Vespa accident silenced their laughter forever. The Aman Palace, once a sanctuary of bliss, became a scene of heartbreak. A call was made, and the world shifted.

Back home, the grandparents—noble and loving though they were—stood shaken. The grandfather, his body weary from strokes and battles with blood pressure, clutched his chest with worry. The grandmother, though gentle and wise, fought her own dragons of asthma and aching limbs. They had strength, yes, and oceans of love—but the road ahead looked impossibly long, raising two little girls whose parents had vanished like mist.

In that heavy silence, a truth whispered through the walls of the house and the cracks in their hearts.

No one had expected the story to end this way.

The couple had planned for sunshine, scraped knees, for graduations, for birthdays, and weddings. But they had not planned for their absence. They had never written the part of the story where they were not the ones guiding their daughters through life's twists and turns.

And so, this fairytale, like all the best ones, carries a lesson:

The greatest treasure a parent holds is not gold or grandeur, but their children. And while castles may crumble and riches fade, the need to protect that treasure—even in your absence—is eternal.

The moral is simple, yet profound: Plan not only for the dreams you chase, but for the storms you cannot see.

Because the most powerful spell of all is love—and love, wisely prepared, can carry on even when you no longer can.

And so, dear reader, take heed. Make your wishes known. Choose guardians as carefully as you choose bedtime stories. And may your children live happily ever after—safe, cherished, and never left to chance.

> **Reflection:** *If the unthinkable happened, who is financially, physically, and emotionally capable to care for your children?*

Best Interests of the Child

We have all heard the horror stories of both parents dying in plane crashes, car accidents, or fires, only to leave behind young children. When tragedies occur, people often assume that relatives will step in to be the caretakers of the children. In situations where one parent of a married couple dies or becomes incapacitated, it is most common that the child's other parent will retain sole custody unless special circumstances exist. In cases where both parents die or the other parent is estranged from the child, the situation can be more complex.

Unless you leave specific instructions for the custody of your children, the court takes over to decide. A judge will have to decide which relatives should take parental control. A judge can choose a relative to take parental control, who the family would have never wanted to take over the child's care. Additionally, the children can be placed in foster care temporarily until a judge determines custody arrangements. This is because each state has its default law as to who would be the selected caretaker in the absence of instructions in a Will. Most states look to the legal standard of *the best interests of the child* to determine custody. Several factors encompass the best interests that a judge will consider when meeting this standard:

(1) **Relationship to the child(ren)**: A judge will review the potential guardian's relationship with the child, especially since young children need hands-on care.
(2) **Consistency**: Courts generally prefer to keep children in a consistent routine. This includes living arrangements, school or childcare routines, and access to extended family members. Courts will try to reduce relocation across state and city lines, but this is not always possible if the best caretaker(s) live in another state.

(3) **Evidence of parenting ability**: The legal system works to ensure that the adult who receives custody meets the child's physical and emotional needs. This includes long-term support for food, shelter, clothing, medical care, education, emotional support, and guidance until the children turn 18 years of age.
(4) **Health**: Courts consider the caretaker's physical and mental health and want to ensure there are no issues with safety, mistreatment, alcohol, or drug abuse.
(5) **Preference**: Very often, children can request who they wish to be their guardian if the judge believes the choice is reasonable.

Despite the court system doing its best to find a suitable caretaker, it often does not get it right. Family courts are inundated with cases and lack resources and personnel to adequately determine the best interests of the child. Judges often must decide quickly where a child would end up to move on to the next case. It would be a mistake for you to think the courts can determine what is best for your children.

You want your children to be protected, and appointing a *guardian* is one of the best ways to show you love them. Therefore, an estate plan that names your preference for a legal guardian is crucial should a tragedy occur. First responders are usually able to place the children with either a family member or the person named in a legal document. It is also advisable to inform the potential guardian that if you were to pass away, you wish for them to take care of your children. This is to avoid the surprise of imposing parenting on those who do not have children and/or did not expect to be nominated as a guardian.

Without a legal guardian in place, schools and medical providers often face significant legal limitations when it comes to making decisions on behalf of the child. For example, schools may be unable to proceed with critical actions such as enrolling the child, implementing or modifying an Individualized Education Program (IEP), or approving participation in extracurricular activities or field trips, all of which typically require a parent or legal guardian's consent. Similarly, doctors and hospitals may not be able to provide non-emergency medical treatment without authorization from a legal guardian or court-appointed representative. These limitations can result in delays in care, interruptions in education, and emotional distress for the child—challenges that could often be avoided if a guardian had been named in advance through a Will or other legal document.

Once decided in the Will, this potential guardian is then responsible for the well-being of the child. The courts will generally follow your wishes and appoint the person designated. The exception would be if the court finds that it is not in the child's best interests to appoint the named guardian. I would venture to go one step further and plan for short-term or temporary guardians and permanent guardians. I suggest you select people who can be there to take the children immediately, but for a temporary period. This is especially prudent if the person you have appointed lives out of state or out of the country. You may consider naming a temporary guardian who can provide immediate caretaking and keep the children out of the government system until the permanent guardian arrives. Temporary guardians can also step in for you if you are hospitalized or stranded while traveling as what occurred during the COVID-19 pandemic.

In summary, when an estate plan does not name a guardian for minor children, the court will choose one. In most cases, a family member steps forward, and everyone interested in being appointed will have a chance to plead their case in court. If there is no surviving family or no one steps forward, it would be up to the government to place the children in a facility or foster care.

The care of your children in the immediate weeks after a disaster like losing their parents is vital. Who can immediately be there to show support, make sure that they are fed and cared for following a traumatic experience, is crucial. Therefore, it is prudent that you, as a parent, select both short-term and long-term guardians as part of your comprehensive estate plan. This next statement is certainly not legal advice, but I am offering it nonetheless: as you contemplate selecting a guardian for your minor children in your stead, I highly recommend you select someone who reflects values that align with what you want instilled in your children. While you may think the "cool" auntie is suitable, she may not foster the values that you care to instill in your children.

Dangerous Designations: Why Your IRA Should Not Go to Your Children

While naming a guardian ensures that your children are cared for physically and emotionally, it is also important to consider how they will be provided for financially. One of the most common mistakes parents make is naming minor children as direct beneficiaries of their estate, without realizing that children cannot legally inherit property outright. If you name your minor child as a beneficiary on your life insurance policy or IRA, the insurance company cannot issue a payment directly to a child under 18 years old. Likewise, adding a minor child's name to your real estate deed is inadvisable because a child cannot legally manage the property, often triggering costly court oversight and limiting your ability to protect or control the asset. Alternatively, you can designate another adult, such as a trustee, to manage funds or real estate on their behalf until they are adults. If you do not legally designate a trustee or guardian to manage money or property for your minor children, the court will appoint someone. This person is often referred to as a conservator or guardian of the estate. The court will supervise how the funds are used, typically requiring regular reports and approval for significant financial decisions. However, there is a risk that the court may appoint someone who is not financially competent, which could result in the mismanagement or squandering of your children's inheritance. When your children turn 18, they can then terminate the conservatorship and receive a lump sum of the remaining money to use as they wish. Placing assets in a trust with your children named as beneficiaries when they reach a certain age is more ideal because it allows the funds to be distributed slowly over time.

The Gift of Time: Why Waiting to Pass on Wealth is Wiser

Parents have always wrestled with the question: When is the right time to pass on wealth? History, culture, and even ancient proverbs remind us that timing can make all the difference. The idea that wealth tends to disappear within a few generations is recognized in many cultures worldwide, often expressed through unique proverbs or sayings. Here are some notable examples: There is a Chinese proverb that warns, "Wealth does not last beyond three generations" (财不外露三), which closely mirrors the American saying, "Shirtsleeves to shirtsleeves in three generations." In Italian, there is the phrase "Da capo alla fine" (from start to finish), often used to describe the cycle of poverty and wealth repeating across generations, especially in family-owned businesses. All these expressions relay timeless truths: without careful planning and education, family wealth often disappears quickly.

Even though a child may legally be an adult, without proper financial education and maturity, he/she may not be responsible or knowledgeable enough to manage inherited assets. Children who inherit significant assets at a young age often lack the maturity, financial knowledge, and life experience to manage them wisely, increasing the risk that the assets will be quickly spent, mismanaged, or lost to bad decisions or outside influences. Many people assume that leaving a financial inheritance to their children or grandchildren will secure their future and give their children comfort, but statistics tell a cautionary tale. Studies show that 70% of wealthy families lose their wealth by the second generation, and 90% by the third.[10] In a widely cited study from Ohio State University, researchers found that the average inheritance is completely spent within five years.[11] Another survey revealed that one in three people who receive an inheritance squander it within two years.[12] These outcomes are often due to a lack of financial literacy, poor spending habits, emotional spending after the death of a loved one, or falling victim to financial predators.

Therefore, even if a child is legally an adult, they may not have the maturity or knowledge to manage a sudden windfall responsibly. As a result, many estate planners recommend using trusts and structured distributions to preserve assets across generations and ensure that inheritances support—rather than endanger—the beneficiary's long-term financial well-being.

---

[10] The Williams Group. "Preparing Heirs: Five Steps to a Successful Transition of Family Wealth and Values."

[11] Jay L. Zagorsky, "Do people save or spend their inheritances? Understanding what happens to inherited wealth," *Journal of Family and Economic Issues*, 2012.

[12] U.S. Consumer Financial Protection Bureau and financial behavior studies reported by MarketWatch, Forbes, and financial advisory firms.

Several famous families illustrate "shirtsleeves to shirtsleeves in three generations." In the United States, the Vanderbilt family rose to prominence under Cornelius "Commodore" Vanderbilt (1794–1877), who amassed one of the largest fortunes of the 19th century through shipping and railroads. His son, William Henry Vanderbilt, doubled that fortune, but by the early 1900s–1930s, the third generation had largely squandered it on palatial estates, lavish lifestyles, and social rivalry. By the 1970s, not a single Vanderbilt appeared among America's wealthiest families.[13]

The Astors, America's first great real estate dynasty, grew from the vision of John Jacob Astor (1763–1848), who became the nation's first multi-millionaire in the early 1800s through fur trading and Manhattan real estate. His descendants, such as William Backhouse Astor Sr. and Jr., maintained the fortune into the mid-19th century, but by the 1900s–1920s, the family's immense holdings had been diluted by inheritance divisions and extravagance. The Astors remained socially prominent but no longer wielded the financial power that once made them America's preeminent dynasty.[14]

---

[13] Arthur T. Vanderbilt II, *Fortune's Children: The Fall of the House of Vanderbilt* (New York: William Morrow/HarperCollins, 1989; reprint eds. thereafter)

[14] Anderson Cooper and Katherine Howe, Astor: The Rise and Fall of an American Fortune (New York: Harper, 2023). David Sinclair, Dynasty: The Astors and Their Times (London: J. M. Dent & Sons, 1983).

The Guggenheim family made their fortune later in the late 1800s, when Meyer Guggenheim (1828–1905) built a mining and smelting empire in Colorado and beyond. His seven sons expanded it into one of the most powerful industrial fortunes in the world. Yet by the 1940s–1960s, the family's wealth had fragmented through multiple heirs and shifting industries. While their concentrated fortune dwindled, their name endured through philanthropy, particularly in the arts, with the creation of the Solomon R. Guggenheim Foundation and its renowned museums.[15]

Across the Atlantic, European aristocratic families suffered a more gradual decline. Many had amassed vast estates over centuries, but beginning in the late 1800s and accelerating through the early-to-mid 1900s, heavy inheritance taxes, land reforms, and the devastation of World War I and World War II made maintaining great houses and fortunes impossible. In Britain, for instance, hundreds of stately homes were abandoned, sold, or demolished between the 1920s and 1950s, marking the end of aristocratic financial dominance.[16]

---

[15] Irwin Unger and Debi Unger, *The Guggenheims: A Family History* (New York: HarperCollins/Harper Perennial, 2005)

[16] David Cannadine, *The Decline and Fall of the British Aristocracy* (New Haven: Yale University Press, 1990; later eds. Penguin). Authoritative study on taxation, land, and status decline c. 1880–1950s. Roy Strong, Marcus Binney, and John Harris (eds.), *The Destruction of the Country House, 1875–1975* (London: Thames & Hudson, 1974) — landmark V&A exhibition catalogue documenting demolitions and fiscal pressures. James Raven (ed.), *Lost Mansions: Essays on the Destruction of the Country*

A more modern example comes from Italy: the Gucci family. Guccio Gucci (1881–1953) founded his Florence leather shop in 1921, and his sons Aldo, Rodolfo, and Vasco expanded it into a global luxury brand by the 1950s–1970s. By the third generation, however, bitter family feuds, lawsuits, and poor management eroded the company's stability. Maurizio Gucci, Rodolfo's son, sold the family's remaining stake in 1993, ending the Gucci family ownership entirely.[17]

This cycle of acquisition and loss of wealth is known as the wealth dissipation cycle or simply the intergenerational wealth transfer challenge. This phenomenon is echoed in various cultures and underscores the challenges of preserving family wealth across multiple generations without proper financial planning, education, or stewardship. Comprehensive estate planning embodies tools that prevent assets from being squandered and lost due to frivolous behavior and misunderstandings about money.

House (London: Palgrave Macmillan, 2015) — scholarly essays that contextualize the 20th-century losses.

[17] Sara Gay Forden, *The House of Gucci: A True Story of Murder, Madness, Glamour, and Greed* (New York: HarperCollins, 2000; updated eds. 2021).

Takeaways

(1) Name a guardian in your Will to avoid court battles over custody.

(2) Avoid naming minors as direct beneficiaries—use a trust to manage their inheritance.

(3) Inheritances left to young adults are often squandered; trusts can stagger distributions.

(4) Financial education is key to breaking the "wealth dissipation cycle" (70% of inheritances are gone by the second generation).

Chapter 5:
The Rest of the Story: Estate Planning Beyond Wills and Trusts

Wills and trusts often take center stage in estate planning, but they are only part of the story. A complete estate plan also prepares for incapacity, streamlines asset distribution, and ensures your personal wishes are honored in every area of life. This chapter will explore the other essential pieces of a well-rounded estate plan—tools that work alongside your Will and trust to protect you and your loved ones.

Let us pause for a moment... *Who would make your healthcare decisions if you were on life support? Do you have someone you trust to manage your finances if you were incapacitated? Would your family know your wishes if you were in a coma?*

Power of Attorney (POA)

A Power of Attorney (POA) is a foundational component of an estate plan that authorizes someone you select—known as your agent or attorney-in-fact—to manage your financial and legal affairs if you become unable to do so. A POA allows someone to act on your behalf, but the authority depends on whether it is *durable* or *non-durable*. A non-durable power of attorney is valid only while you remain competent, and it automatically ends if you become incapacitated, making it most useful for limited or short-term matters such as handling a single financial transaction. By contrast, a durable power of attorney includes special language that allows it to remain effective even if you later lose capacity, ensuring your agent can continue managing your affairs, paying bills, or making legal decisions on your behalf. The key distinction is that a non-durable POA loses its authority, while a durable POA continues, making its durable status a central tool in estate and long-term care planning.

POAs can grant broad authority over your affairs, or restrict authority to specific tasks or timeframes, such as selling a property while you are overseas. Also, a springing POA only becomes effective once a physician declares you incapacitated, offering an extra layer of control. It is wise to appoint both a primary and a backup agent, and to update the document regularly to ensure financial institutions continue to honor it. Without a valid POA, your loved ones may have to go through a lengthy and costly court process to gain control of your assets should you become incapacitated.

Healthcare Directives

Healthcare directives ensure your medical preferences are respected when you cannot advocate for yourself. The two most common documents are a *Living Will* and a *Healthcare Power of Attorney* (sometimes called a *Healthcare Proxy*). A living will outlines the types of life-sustaining treatments you do or do not want in circumstances such as terminal illness or permanent unconsciousness, such as ventilators, feeding tubes, and resuscitation. The healthcare power of attorney designates someone to make medical decisions on your behalf if you are unable to do so. This person should be someone who understands your values and can handle stressful decisions. Also, including HIPAA authorization language in this document is important to ensure your healthcare agent has full access to your medical records to make reasonable healthcare decisions. Together, these documents provide both clarity and authority, reducing the burden on family members during medical emergencies and emotional and uncertain times.

Beneficiary Designations

Beneficiary designations are often overlooked but an essential part of estate planning because they govern the distribution of certain assets independently of your Will or trust. When beneficiaries are appropriately selected, accounts such as retirement plans (including IRAs and 401(k)s), life insurance policies, and payable-on-death bank accounts may pass directly to the individuals named as beneficiaries. This transfer is typically fast and bypasses the probate process. However, it is crucial that these designations are consistent with your broader estate plan. For instance, naming one child as the sole beneficiary of a life insurance policy, while intending your estate to be divided equally, could create unintended disparities. These designations should be reviewed regularly—especially after major life events such as marriage, divorce, births, or deaths—to ensure they still reflect your intentions and do not inadvertently override your Will.

Guardianship Designations

As discussed in the previous chapter, guardianship designations are essential if you have minor children or dependents who require ongoing care. These are usually included in your Will and nominate a person—or people—you trust to raise your children should something happen to you and the other parent. The court has the final say, but your nomination carries significant weight. You can also name separate individuals to serve as guardians of the person (day-to-day caregiving) and of the estate (financial management), which can be helpful in families where one person is more nurturing and another more financially savvy. If you have a dependent with special needs, you may need to plan for lifelong care, including appointing a guardian for adulthood and creating a special needs trust to preserve eligibility for public benefits. These designations should be updated as your children grow and as circumstances among potential guardians evolve.

Digital Asset Planning

Digital asset planning is an increasingly important yet frequently overlooked element of modern estate planning. It involves organizing and securing access to your digital property—such as email accounts, social media profiles, the course you created, cloud storage, online banking, and cryptocurrency. Without proper planning, your executor may struggle to access or manage these assets, and valuable or sentimental content could be lost. Many platforms now allow you to designate a legacy contact or assign access through built-in tools, but you should also include clear instructions in your estate documents authorizing your representatives to handle your digital affairs. Maintaining a secure list of usernames, passwords, two-factor authentication methods, and the location of any hardware wallets or recovery keys is essential. This list should be stored securely—such as in a password manager or encrypted file—and made accessible to a trusted individual, often called a "digital executor." Addressing these assets proactively prevents confusion and ensures that nothing important is left behind.

Letter of Intent

A letter of intent, though not a legally binding document, serves as a valuable supplement to your estate plan. It is a written statement to your executor, loved ones, or beneficiaries, offering personal insights into your wishes that are not addressed in formal legal documents. This might include guidance on funeral or memorial preferences, the reasoning behind specific bequests, or values you wish to pass down to your heirs. In some cases, it can also contain information about your digital life—such as instructions for social media accounts or online subscriptions. Because it is not legally binding, the letter of intent offers flexibility in both tone and content, and it can be updated informally as your preferences change. Many families find that it provides emotional clarity and reduces confusion during a difficult time.

Funeral and Final Arrangements

While funeral preferences can be included in a letter of intent, some individuals create a separate document specifically addressing final arrangements. This might include choices such as burial or cremation, preferred funeral home, desired religious or cultural rituals, or even a prepaid funeral plan. These instructions are not legally binding, but they offer tremendous relief to grieving loved ones who would otherwise be left guessing. Documenting these wishes clearly—and sharing them with your family or executor—can help ensure that your final send-off reflects your values.

Estate Plan Organization and Storage

No matter how carefully you craft your estate plan, it is effective only if the right people can find the right documents when they are needed. Store your estate planning documents—including your Will, Trust, Powers of Attorney, Healthcare Directives, and digital access instructions—in a secure but accessible place. This might be a fireproof safe, a secure cloud-based vault, or a binder kept with your attorney. Let your executor, trustee, and key family members know where to find everything. Some individuals maintain a "master file" or "family emergency binder" with key instructions, contacts, and copies of essential paperwork.

While Wills and Trusts are essential, they are just two pieces of the estate planning puzzle. The mentioned documents and your digital footprint all play a role in ensuring your wishes are carried out smoothly and with minimal burden on your loved ones. By taking the time to address each of these components, you are creating a plan that is not only comprehensive, but also compassionate.

> **Reflection:** *If you were unable to make decisions for yourself, who would have the legal authority to speak or act on your behalf?*

Chapter 6:
A Debt to Remember: What Happens to Your Financial Commitments When You Are Gone?

In addition to concerns about inheritance and legal responsibilities, many families are unsure how a loved one's financial obligations are handled after death. One of the most common and emotional questions I receive after the death of a loved one is, "What happens to their debt, and am I responsible for paying it?" This is a stressful and confusing time, and unfortunately, misinformation spreads quickly. The short answer is no. You are generally not personally responsible for someone else's debt simply because you are related to them. In this chapter, I will explain the key factors that determine how debts are handled after death, including:

- ⇒ How to handle credit card debt
- ⇒ How to deal with debt collectors
- ⇒ How to handle medical debts
- ⇒ What happens when you inherit a property with a mortgage
- ⇒ What happens when a person dies with a reverse mortgage

Credit Card Debt

Under the Fair Debt Collection Practices Act (FDCPA), creditors are prohibited from using deceptive, threatening, or harassing tactics to pressure surviving family members into paying a deceased person's debts—unless those family members are legally responsible, such as co-signers or joint account holders. While debt collectors are allowed to contact the surviving spouse, executor, administrator, or personal representative to discuss outstanding credit card or commercial debts, they cannot require these individuals to pay the debts from their own personal funds—unless one of a few specific exceptions applies. These exceptions typically include being a co-signer on the account, a joint account holder, or living in a community property state, where spouses may be held liable for certain debts incurred during the marriage.

Simply being related to the deceased, or being an authorized user on a credit card, does not make someone personally liable. Credit card companies *may* contact these loved ones to collect information about a debt. Creditors who want to collect from an estate must file a formal claim through the probate court. They cannot satisfy debts simply by contacting family members or asking them to pay voluntarily.

Also, before you get anxious to pay credit card debt, you want to verify the statute of limitations on how long creditors can pursue payment after death. For example, in California, the statute of limitations is one year after the debtor's death for the creditor to try to satisfy a debt. In New York, creditors have only seven months after an executor/administrator is appointed to file a claim against an estate. Therefore, creditors have a short timeframe to bring a claim against the estate. Once that period has passed, the estate is no longer responsible for the debt, and the creditor loses the right to collect on the debt. Best practice: Families should never pay estate debts out of personal funds unless they are certain they are legally responsible. Instead, debts should be handled by the executor/personal representative through the estate.

How to Handle Debt Collectors of Deceased Loved Ones

Simply because you are not responsible for paying the debt does not mean you ignore it. If you are managing the estate, you should gather all the creditors' information and inform them **in writing** that your loved one has passed away. This is typically a letter that you can write to them informing them of the passing, along with an original death certificate that you will mail or email to them (*See Sample Letter Appendix A*). Most credit card companies and banks will want to see a death certificate to close out an account. This is why I recommend that executors obtain multiple copies of death certificates to provide to different entities when requested.

If you are a loved one of the deceased and hold a joint card, it is important that you do not use the card until you have notified the company of the death. This especially applies to any card where the deceased was the sole account holder. Even if you are an authorized user of a card, it is technically fraudulent to continue using it after the primary cardholder's death.

Thieves Look Through Obituaries

Another important reason to notify credit card issuers and lenders of a recent passing—is to protect loved ones against later financial and legal issues regarding an outstanding debt. This is especially important if surviving loved ones hold joint accounts. Additionally, identity thieves commonly target deceased cardholders by searching for obituaries and recent death records in the hopes of snagging a name with unprotected data to hijack. In addition to directly contacting credit card companies, family members or the executor can also help prevent fraudulent use by contacting one of the three main credit report bureaus—Equifax, Experian, and TransUnion—to freeze the deceased's credit. This step may prevent identity thieves from accessing the private credit history of the deceased and prevent their ability to open new accounts under the deceased's name. These credit bureaus require a copy of the death certificate and the Social Security number (SSN) of the deceased to close out the account.

Medical Debts and Filial Responsibility

In some states, under *filial responsibility* laws, children can be held accountable for their parents' medical bills *post mortem* (after death). Filial responsibility laws impose a legal obligation on adult children to pay for their parents' basic needs and medical care. Although most people are unaware, as of 2025, 29 states in the U.S. have some form of filial responsibility law in place. The states that have such laws are Alaska, Arkansas, California, Connecticut, Delaware, Georgia, Indiana, Iowa, Kentucky, Louisiana, Maryland, Massachusetts, Mississippi, Montana, Nevada, New Hampshire, New Jersey, North Carolina, North Dakota, Ohio, Oregon, Pennsylvania, Rhode Island, South Dakota, Tennessee, Utah, Vermont, Virginia and West Virginia.

Filial responsibility laws and their enforcement vary significantly by state. While 29 states and Puerto Rico have such laws on the books, most are rarely enforced, and at least 11 states have never enforced them. Pennsylvania is the most notable for active enforcement, with limited evidence of aggressive application in South Dakota and Puerto Rico. One key reason these laws are not widely used is that, under federal Medicaid law, a parent's eligibility for Medicaid Long-Term Care benefits cannot be affected by the income or assets of anyone other than a spouse. This means states may not require adult children to contribute financially for their parents to qualify for Medicaid Long-Term Care. However, filial responsibility laws may still apply outside the Medicaid context—such as when a parent is receiving care in a private-pay facility and cannot pay—and adult children may be held liable in those situations, depending on the state's enforcement practices.

What if I Die Before Paying Off My House?

Unlike medical or personal debts, which may raise questions about a family member's liability, mortgage debt is treated differently because it is tied directly to the property itself. To understand how mortgage debt is handled after death, it is important to first distinguish how it functions in relation to property ownership. The deed and the mortgage are two separate legal instruments: the deed establishes ownership of the property, while the mortgage represents a loan secured by that property (a person can be responsible for one and not the other).

When a homeowner dies, the deed determines who owns the property, but the mortgage remains a debt attached to the home, not the person. If there is a Will or trust, the property ownership is transferred to the named heir; the heir then owns the home. That person can also continue the mortgage payments if she wishes to keep the home, even if the mortgage is not in his/her name. If there is no Will, the property also goes through probate, and the deed is transferred according to state intestacy laws, typically to the closest relatives. In both cases, the mortgage must still be paid even if the heir is not responsible for the mortgage—inheritance of the home does not erase the debt, and failure to make payments can result in foreclosure. Even while the property is in probate, the mortgage must continue to be paid to avoid foreclosure.

Inheriting a Mortgaged Property: What You Need to Know

If you inherit a property that has a mortgage, although you may not be personally liable on the loan, the property is still subject to the mortgage lien. However, there are a few ways to manage your newfound asset. Federal and state laws generally require mortgage servicers to work with surviving spouses or heirs who inherit mortgaged property. However, the terms vary by loan type and state law. FHA-insured loans have specific protections for surviving spouses when the spouse was a co-borrower. Private loans or conventional mortgages are less flexible, and the lender's willingness to work with heirs can vary. They are generally required to follow foreclosure and loan servicing laws, but are not obligated to offer special terms.

When you inherit a home with an existing mortgage, you can continue making the payments if you wish to keep the property. However, you do not automatically become personally liable for the loan unless you formally assume the mortgage or refinance it in your own name. That said, you are not required to refinance or assume the mortgage to live in the home; if the payments continue, the lender will generally allow you to stay, even if the mortgage remains in the deceased person's name.

Assuming the Mortgage

Some mortgages are *assumable*, meaning the heir can take over the existing loan under its current terms. This is more common with FHA, VA, or USDA loans, but some conventional loans may allow assumption as well. To determine whether assumption is an option, you should contact the loan servicer to ask about eligibility, fees, and qualification requirements. **The ability to assume a mortgage is not based on state law—it is based on the type of loan and the lender's terms.** Even if assumption is not possible or required, heirs are generally allowed to continue making payments to avoid foreclosure, especially if they plan to reside in the home. Under federal law, lenders cannot demand full repayment solely due to the borrower's death if the property is inherited by a family member who occupies the home.

If the existing mortgage is not assumable or you choose not to assume it, you may refinance the loan into your own name. Refinancing is subject to standard lending requirements, including a credit check, income verification, and meeting the lender's ability-to-repay criteria under federal lending laws.

Alternatively, as the heir, you have the option to sell the property and use the proceeds to pay off the existing mortgage. After the loan is satisfied, any remaining funds belong to the estate and will be distributed to the heirs according to the Will or state intestacy laws if there is no Will.

What Happens to a Reverse Mortgage When a Borrower Dies?

In addition to traditional mortgages, some heirs may inherit homes with a *reverse mortgage*, which operates quite differently and has unique implications after the homeowner's death. A reverse mortgage is a special type of loan available to homeowners age 62 or older that allows them to borrow money using their home's equity—without having to make monthly mortgage payments. It allows seniors to turn part of their home's value into cash while still living in the home. The loan is repaid only when the homeowner moves out, sells the home, or passes away. Here are the scenarios with leaving behind a reverse mortgage:

(1) **Heirs Repay the Loan and Keep the Home**: The heirs can choose to pay off the reverse mortgage loan balance (including interest and fees) to keep the home. Typically, they can do this by refinancing the loan or using other funds. Once the loan is repaid, they gain full ownership of the property free and clear.

(2) **Heirs Sell the Home to Repay the Loan**: If the heirs do not want to keep the home or cannot afford to repay the loan, they can sell the property. The proceeds from the sale first go to paying off the reverse mortgage. Any remaining funds after the loan is fully repaid belong to the heirs or estate.

(3) Heirs Do Nothing and the Lender Forecloses: If the heirs do not repay the loan or sell the home within a certain timeframe (usually 6-12 months after the homeowner's death), the lender may initiate foreclosure proceedings to recover the loan amount. The heirs lose ownership, and the lender sells the home.

(4) Heirs Surrender the Property to the Lender: Heirs can choose to surrender the home voluntarily to the lender as full repayment of the reverse mortgage. This means the lender takes ownership of the property, and the heirs walk away without further financial responsibility.

Takeaways:

(1) Survivors, including spouses, are generally not personally responsible for the deceased's debts unless they were co-signers, joint account holders, or otherwise legally liable.
(2) Creditors and debt collectors cannot legally coerce survivors into paying a deceased person's debts unless the survivors share legal responsibility.
(3) Mortgage servicers typically work with heirs, but specific terms and processes vary depending on the loan type and state law.
(4) Assuming the mortgage may be possible. If assumption is not an option, refinancing under your own name requires qualification but can offer better terms.

(5) Selling the inherited home to pay off the mortgage or reverse mortgage is always an option.

(6) You can continue living in a home you inherit and make payments on the mortgage even if the loan remains in the deceased's name.

(7) When inheriting a home with a reverse mortgage, heirs can:

    (a) Repay the loan and keep the home,

    (b) Sell the home to pay off the loan,

    (c) Surrender the home to the lender, or

    (d) Risk foreclosure if no action is taken.

Chapter 7:
What Taxes Are Due When a Person Dies?

Founding father of the United States of America, Benjamin Franklin, famously noted that only two things are certain: death and taxes. Estate taxes, sometimes referred to as "death taxes," combine them both. Death taxes refer to the tax that is applied on the transfer of a deceased person's assets to their heirs or beneficiaries. The tax is calculated based on the value of the estate at the time of death, including all property, investments, real estate, cash, and other assets. Imagine that at the time of your death, a snapshot is taken of all the assets you own or in which you have a financial interest. These assets, regardless of their location, constitute your gross estate for estate tax purposes. The IRS considers the following types of assets when calculating the total value of an estate:

⇒ Real property
⇒ Stocks and bonds
⇒ Cash and bank accounts
⇒ Life insurance or annuity interests
⇒ Retirement accounts (e.g., 401(k)s, IRAs)
⇒ Personal property, including vehicles, clothing, and household furnishings

While the estate tax focuses on the value of the assets left behind, beneficiaries must also be aware of the taxes they may face upon receiving those assets. To fully understand the financial impact, it is important to recognize the tax implications that can arise when inheriting property or other assets. An inheritance may trigger several types of taxes, depending on the nature of the asset, how it was passed on, and the applicable federal or state laws. This section provides an overview of the key taxes, beneficiaries may encounter, including capital gains tax, income tax on trust distributions, and estate or inheritance taxes. Understanding these obligations can help beneficiaries make informed decisions and avoid unexpected taxes.

Capital Gains Tax

When inheriting certain assets, beneficiaries should consider *capital gain taxes*. A capital gains tax is a tax imposed on capital assets. A capital asset is a long-term asset that provides future economic benefits and is typically "held" for more than one year. Taxes are imposed on the profit made when a capital asset is sold for more than its original cost. This tax applies regardless of whether the asset is passed through a Will, a trust, or without a Will. However, it is important to understand that inherited capital assets typically receive a *step-up in basis*—meaning the asset's value is adjusted to its fair market value at the time of the decedent's death. As a result, the original purchase price is disregarded, which can significantly reduce—or even eliminate—capital gains tax if the beneficiary sells the asset shortly after inheriting it. A sale, soon after the death of the original owner, ensures that the value of the asset does not increase too much, subjecting the beneficiary to too much tax. However, not all assets qualify for this step-up.

Common Examples of Capital Assets
- ⇒ Real estate (e.g., your home, rental property, land)
- ⇒ Stocks, bonds, crypto, and other investments
- ⇒ Personal property (e.g., cars, jewelry, art) if sold for a gain
- ⇒ Collectables (e.g., rare coins, vintage wine)

Common Examples of Non-Capital Assets:
- ⇒ Personal items sold at a loss (e.g., your couch, clothes)
- ⇒ Inventory (if you are a business owner selling goods)

For example, if you inherit a house, its value is stepped-up to the fair market value on the date of the original owner's death. This stepped-up value becomes your new cost basis. If you sell the house shortly after inheriting it—typically within 6 to 12 months—there may be little or no increase in value, so you might owe minimal or no capital gains tax. However, if you keep the house for several years and its value rises significantly, you could owe capital gains tax on the difference between the stepped-up basis and the sale price.

Capital gains tax is triggered only when the asset is sold, not when it is simply inherited. So, holding onto the property does not create an immediate tax liability, but it can increase your eventual tax exposure if the asset appreciates in value over time. The following illustration should help you understand how step-up basis works.

The Tale of Princess Penny and the Magic Cottage

Once upon a time, in a cozy kingdom, there lived a kind old Queen named Rose. She owned a little cottage in the woods that she bought long ago for just a $1 gold coin. Years later, the cottage was worth $10 gold coins because it was so charming and special. When Queen Rose grew very old, she gave the cottage to her granddaughter, Princess Penny, in her Will. Queen Rose passed away peacefully, and Penny inherited the cottage. Now here is the magic part: when Queen Rose passed, the royal tax fairies gave the cottage a "step-up" spell. That spell changed the value of the cottage in the royal records to $10 gold coins—the amount it was worth on the day Queen Rose died. So, when Princess Penny sold the cottage a few weeks later for $10 gold coins, the tax fairies smiled and said, "No tax today! You did not make any extra gold." But if there had not been a step-up spell, the kingdom would have said Penny made $9 gold coins from the sale—and taxed her! And that is why the step-up in basis is such a helpful magic rule when you inherit something.

Taxes on Trusts

In addition to potential capital gains taxes on inherited assets, beneficiaries should also be aware of how taxes apply to assets held in a trust. Trust beneficiaries typically pay taxes payouts they receive from the trust's income—such as interest, dividends, or rental income—while distributions from the principal (the original amount placed into the trust) are generally not taxable. That is because the IRS considers principal funds used to establish a trust to be previously taxed money or contributions made with after-tax dollars. Whether a trust's income is taxed to the trust itself or passed to the beneficiaries depends on how the trust is structured and whether the trust retains or distributes its income. If the trust distributes income to beneficiaries, it passes the tax responsibility to them and deducts the amount distributed from its own tax return. Beneficiaries receive a Schedule K-1 from the trust, which shows the types and amounts of income they must report on their own tax returns. The K-1 distinguishes between taxable income (like interest or dividends) and nontaxable principal distributions. Since principal distributions do not represent new income, the IRS does not treat them as a taxable event.[18]

Estate Taxes

As of 2025, the Internal Revenue Service (IRS) applies a federal estate tax exemption to estates valued below $13.99 million per individual or $27.98 million for married couples. This means that only estates exceeding these thresholds will be subject to the federal estate tax when transferred to heirs. Assets below these

---

[18]"Schedule K-1 Federal Tax Form: What Is It and Who Is It For?" *Investopedia*, 7 June 2010, www.investopedia.com/terms/s/schedule-k-1.asp.
The K-1 form is also used to report income distributions from trusts and estates to beneficiaries. A Schedule K-1 document is prepared for each relevant beneficiary.

limits can be passed to heirs free of federal estate taxes, allowing many high-net-worth families to transfer substantial wealth without tax liability. Only the amount of the estate that exceeds these limits is subject to federal estate tax, not the full value of the estate.

However, this generous exemption is set to decrease. Under current law, the Tax Cuts and Jobs Act (TCJA) provisions, enacted in 2017 will sunset after 2025, causing the exemption to revert to pre-TCJA levels, estimated at around $7 million per individual. This change will significantly reduce the amount that can be passed tax-free, potentially exposing more estates to taxation.

When someone dies and leaves assets to their spouse, no estate tax is typically due because of the *unlimited marital deduction*, which allows tax-free transfers between spouses. However, those assets are then included in the surviving spouse's estate, and may be taxed upon their death. If the surviving spouse remarries, he/she can still use the marital deduction with their new spouse. Additionally, assets left to qualified charitable organizations are not subject to estate tax, regardless of marital status.

Are There State Estate Taxes, Too?

In addition to the federal estate tax, some states impose their own estate or inheritance taxes. This means that even if your estate is below the federal exemption amount ($13.99 million per individual and $27.98 million for married couples in 2025), your assets could still be taxed by your state when you pass away.

State Estate Taxes Come in Two Forms:

⇒ **State Estate Tax**
- **Who Pays**: The estate pays the tax before assets are distributed to heirs.
- **Based On**: The location of the decedent.
- **Applies Before Distribution**: The tax is deducted from the total estate, reducing what is passed to beneficiaries.
- **State Examples**: Oregon, Massachusetts, New York, Washington, and others.

⇒ **Inheritance Tax**
- **Who Pays**: The individual beneficiaries pay the tax after receiving their inheritance.
- **Based On**: The residence of the heir, not the decedent.
- **Rates Vary**: Close relatives (e.g., spouses, children) often pay **nothing or lower rates**, while distant relatives or unrelated individuals may pay more.
- **State Examples**: Five states have an inheritance tax — Kentucky, Maryland, Nebraska, New Jersey, and Pennsylvania.

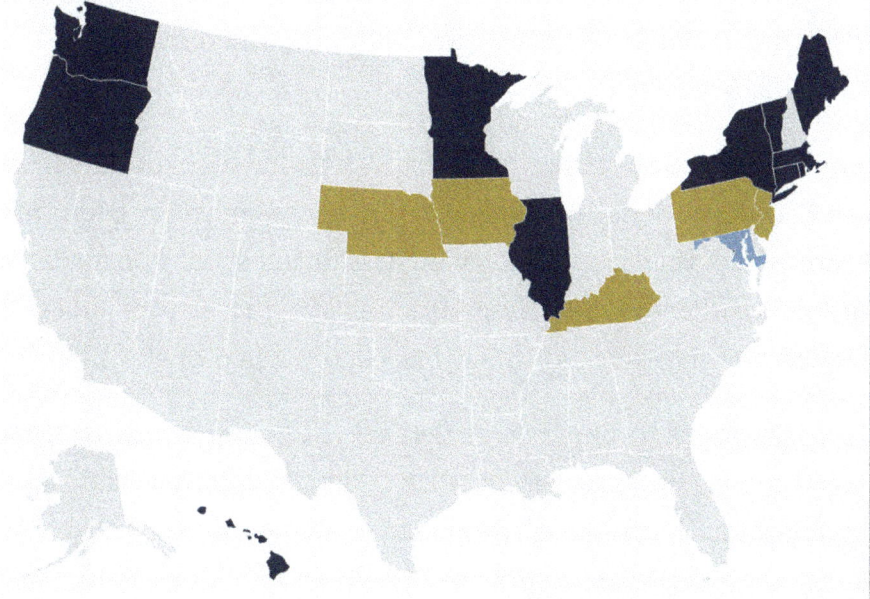

> **Reflection:** *Could your beneficiaries face surprise tax bills?*

---

[19] **Tax Foundation.** "Does Your State Have an Estate or Inheritance Tax? State Estate & Inheritance Tax Rates and Exemptions in 2024." *Tax Foundation*, 2024, www.taxfoundation.org/estate-inheritance-tax-map-2024/. Accessed 16 Oct. 2025.

Who Is Responsible for Making Sure These Taxes Are Paid?

The executor or the trustee is responsible for filing the applicable federal and state estate tax returns and ensuring that all taxes are paid from the estate. After confirming no additional liabilities exist, the executor or trustee will distribute the remaining assets to the named beneficiaries.

The federal estate tax return, Form 706, is due nine months from the decedent's date of death and can be extended an additional six months. If an estate tax payment is due, it should be made on or before the original filing deadline for the return, unless a request for an extension to pay has been granted by the IRS.

It is important to understand that the IRS can take up to three years to let an executor or trustee know whether they have accepted the return as filed or if they will audit the return. An audit of an estate tax return may result in additional estate taxes being assessed. It is common for several years to have passed before the executor or trustee receives a final assessment from the IRS. Audits of estate tax returns are relatively common, especially for larger estates. This extended review process means that executors or trustees may wait years for the final clearance, as the IRS carefully examines high-value assets, deductions, and reported distributions.

__Savvy Planning to Reduce Estate Taxes__

If your estate is nearing or exceeds the federal or state estate tax exemption threshold, proactive planning can help reduce the potential tax burden and preserve more wealth for your beneficiaries. Below are several common strategies to discuss with your wealth advisor. Most of these involve **irrevocable trusts**. These strategies often require careful coordination with an estate planning attorney and tax advisor. *Please note this is not an exhaustive list, but a sample of approaches commonly used in high-net-worth estate planning.*

__Leave Assets to Charity:__

Donating to a qualified charity—either outright or through a **Charitable Remainder Trust (CRT)**—can significantly reduce or eliminate estate taxes. CRTs allow you to retain an income stream for yourself or others, with the remainder going to charity. All charitable donations from your estate are eligible for the **unlimited charitable deduction**, supporting causes you care about while lowering your taxable estate.

__Establish an Irrevocable Trust__

Transferring assets into an irrevocable trust during your lifetime removes those assets—and any future income or appreciation—from your taxable estate. While this means giving up control over the trust property, the potential reduction in estate taxes can be significant.

Use an Irrevocable Life Insurance Trust (ILIT)

An ILIT holds a life insurance policy outside your estate, meaning the policy is titled to or owned by the irrevocable trust. You contribute funds to the trust by making gifts, usually by check from your regular checking account payable to the Trustee of the ILIT. The Trustee deposits the funds into the bank account belonging to the irrevocable trust. These transfers are treated as gifts for tax purposes. If kept within the annual gift tax exclusion ($18,000 per beneficiary in 2025), you typically avoid gift taxes. The trustee must notify the beneficiaries (via a "Crummey letter") that they have the right to withdraw the funds for a short period. Beneficiaries almost never actually withdraw the money, but the notice makes the gift qualify as a present-interest gift (so it counts under the annual exclusion). After the withdrawal window closes, the trustee uses the gifted money and writes a check from the irrevocable trust bank account that received the gift to pay the life insurance premiums. The grantor never pays the insurance company directly. Money always flows: Grantor → ILIT → Insurance Company. If the IRS ever audits, you have a paper trail showing the trust truly owned and paid for the policy. The trustee controls the bank account and the policy, not the grantor. The death benefit is paid to the ILIT when the insured dies, staying outside the grantor's estate.

Beneficiaries get the payout under the terms you wrote in the ILIT (e.g., staggered ages, education support, etc.).

An **(ILIT)** is often thought of as a "wealthy person's" tool — and in many cases, that is true. But sometimes people with more modest means also use it, depending on their family and financial goals. Even if estate taxes are not an issue, ILITs can still be attractive. Consider the following examples:

⇒ **Asset Protection**: If parents worry about children's divorces, creditors, or poor money management, an ILIT ensures the insurance payout is protected and distributed under controlled terms.

⇒ **Special Needs Planning**: Parents of a child with special needs may use an ILIT to hold insurance so the child receives financial support without losing eligibility for government benefits.

⇒ **Blended Families**: An ILIT can ensure life insurance benefits go to children from a first marriage, while other assets go to a current spouse.

⇒ **Privacy and Control**: Unlike a will, an ILIT is private and does not go through probate. This appeals even to those without taxable estates. Example: A teacher and nurse couple with a $1.2M estate (house and savings) buy a $500k life policy inside an ILIT. At death, the trustee uses proceeds for children's education in a controlled, protected way.

Pay Educational or Medical Expenses Directly

You can make unlimited payments for someone's tuition or qualified medical costs without triggering gift tax, if the payments are made directly to the institution or provider. This is a simple and efficient way to transfer wealth while avoiding both gift and estate taxes.

Because tax laws and exemption amounts can change, it is important to work with a team of professionals—including a wealth advisor, estate planning attorney, and tax specialist—to develop a strategy tailored to your goals. With the right planning, you can reduce taxes and leave a legacy for future generations.

Takeaways:

(1) Capital gains tax is a federal (and sometimes state) tax on the increase in value of a capital asset—such as real estate, stocks, bonds, or valuable collectibles—between the time it was acquired and when it is sold.

(2) There are two types of capital assets: short-term (held less than a year, taxed at higher rates) and long-term (held over a year, taxed at lower rates). You owe taxes on the gain, not the total sale price.

(3) When you inherit property, its value is "stepped-up" to the market value at the owner's death. This means capital gains taxes are calculated from this stepped-up value, often reducing taxes.
(4) Whether property passes through a trust or probate, the step-up applies.
(5) An estate may be subject to federal or state taxes
(6) Capital gains tax is calculated from the death of the original owner of the asset.
(7) There are various tools to protect assets and transfer wealth depending on the goals of the individual.

Chapter 8:
The New American Dream: A Global Journey

Estate planning is one of the most powerful tools for preserving wealth, protecting loved ones' future, and ensuring a smooth transfer of assets from one generation to the next. But true generational wealth is about more than money or documents—it is also about passing down options, security, and freedom. That includes security and the freedom to live well. In today's globalized world, building a legacy can also mean creating pathways for your children or grandchildren to thrive in places where access, affordability, and quality of life are often greater than what is currently available in the United States.

Ask Yourself...Would I be open to receiving high-quality care in another country if it meant preserving more of my savings? Have I ever considered retiring—or aging—in a country where care is more affordable and dignified?

This chapter shifts the focus from estate planning within U.S. borders to a broader vision of opportunity: retiring and relocating abroad. While you can have a solid estate plan in the United States, you may also want to consider what it means to invest in a lifestyle and legacy beyond the U.S.—where your money may go further, your healthcare may be more accessible, and your quality of life may dramatically improve. Whether for financial reasons, health considerations, or a desire for cultural enrichment, moving abroad is not only possible, it is increasingly practical—and for many, it is the smartest decision they can make for their future and their family's future.

After several financial crises over the past two decades, people's ability to retire in the U.S. is more precarious. This is not only due to economic concerns such as inflation, but lack of affordable healthcare, social unrest, the rise in the cost of living, poor quality of life, the rise in crime, political instability and uncertainty, and compounded frustration with the happenings in the United States. People are increasingly despondent with politicians and feel let down by their local and federal governments. The relentless uncertainty has made Americans feel frustrated and desperate.

Moreover, those of retirement age, who have worked for 30, 40, or even 50 years, face the anxiety of not knowing whether they can retire comfortably. America promised its people that if they sacrificed and worked hard, and dedicated themselves to their jobs and paid their bills, they would have time, location, and financial freedom. Upon retirement, when the time comes to "collect" on those promises, many Americans discover that nothing is waiting for them at the end of the proverbial pot. They must continue to struggle despite a lifetime of sacrifice.

Many are fearful that they will not be able to even retire, and expect to work until death. Many more seniors have been forced to reenter the workforce to make ends meet because their social security, pension, and savings are insufficient to live comfortably. For these reasons, retirement in the United States is challenging.

Thankfully, and not yet commonly considered by the masses, retirement abroad is possible, plausible, and highly advisable.

America has been the land of opportunities for many immigrants who have made the long journey and sacrifice of leaving their home country for a "better life" in the United States. However, America has also been experiencing an exodus of Americans leaving for a better life, which some are finding in Latin America, Africa, Asia, and Europe. Who would have thought that other countries—some of which were deemed part of the "developing world"—would be able to offer Americans safety, stability, affordability, affordable healthcare, and culture. Thus, motivating Americans to move their entire families.

So, what is the surprising truth about retiring abroad? Well, there are several countries that allow Americans to retire affordably and comfortably. Offering the comforts Americans are accustomed to while including aspects that have been excluded from Americans (think universal healthcare, free or low-cost higher education, paid maternity leave, robust public transportation, stronger worker and privacy protections, and affordable housing). Many of these countries embody what I call *casual luxury*—not luxury in the sense of excess or extravagance, but in the quiet, consistent presence of dignity, comfort, and beauty in everyday life. It is the ability to visit a clean and welcoming public park, to buy affordable and fresh produce from a local market, to afford a doctor's visit without fear of financial ruin, or to enjoy a slower pace of life where people greet each other in the streets. In these countries, casual luxury means living well without having to be rich. It means experiencing freedom not only in your finances, but in your health, your time, and your environment. For many retirees, this way of life is not only more affordable—it is more fulfilling. These are experiences that should be considered basic human rights—yet in the United States—these basic human needs have increasingly become commodified, making them unattainable for millions of working-class people.

> **Reflection:** *Am I staying in the U.S. because I am used to the lifestyle and routines here, or because living here is truly my best option?*

Healthcare In the United States

The United States ranks last on the list of healthcare systems of the eleven (11) wealthiest countries in the world—despite spending the highest percentage of its Gross Domestic Product (GDP) on healthcare.[20] The country struggles with administrative hurdles, affordability, access, and equity. The important point about the U.S. health disadvantage is not that the United States is losing a competition with other countries, but that Americans are dying and suffering at demonstrably unnecessary rates. The

---

[20]Schneider, Eric C., et al. *Mirror, Mirror 2021: Reflecting Poorly: Health Care in the U.S. Compared to Other High-Income Countries.* Commonwealth Fund, 4 Aug. 2021, www.commonwealthfund.org/publications/fund-reports/2021/aug/mirror-mirror-2021-reflecting-poorly.

healthcare crisis is immense, not because there are no solutions, but because every other rich country has been able to figure out how to help people live longer, healthier lives. That means that Americans could do it too. The changes may not be as hard as some policymakers and health officials seem to think.

When you observe healthier countries like Switzerland, France, Italy, Germany, and Spain, they are all free societies. They are not banning delicious foods or forcing people to do exercise boot camps. Americans love visiting Europe, Australia, and the Caribbean to enjoy the food and lifestyle there. So, suggesting that we adopt some of those healthy habits should not feel like a threat to anyone's liberty. Learning from other countries' policies is simply common sense. There are dozens of countries across almost every continent of the world that have outperformed the United States in healthcare for 50 years because the United States has done little to improve healthcare access and systems.[21] Meanwhile, healthcare costs continue to increase while healthcare standards decrease.

Furthermore, the United States' health disadvantages cannot only be attributed to the health disparities that exist among its various

---

[21] **Centers for Medicare & Medicaid Services.** *National Health Expenditure Data.* U.S. Department of Health and Human Services, 2023, https://www.cms.gov/data-research/statistics-trends-and-reports/national-health-expenditure-data. Shows that the U.S. ranks last among 11 high-income nations in healthcare performance despite the highest spending.

racial and ethnic groups.[22] It is true that policies rooted in systemic racism have produced inequities in health outcomes for disenfranchised groups, Indigenous communities, and people of color.[23] However, even "privileged" white Americans living in the United States experience poorer health compared to those in other countries.[24] Studies show that white Americans have higher mortality rates when compared to white people in Great Britain, and rich Americans die earlier and have more disease than rich people in other countries.[25] What ails America is systemic, and it affects everyone, regardless of race and income. And what drives the stark inequities in health is also systemic to the United States.

---

[22] Deehan, Jeannie. "Social and Economic Policies Can Help Reverse Americans' Declining Health." *Center for American Progress*, 17 Feb. 2025, www.americanprogress.org/article/social-economic-policies-can-help-reverse-americans-declining-health/

[23] Institute of Medicine (US) Committee on Understanding and Eliminating Racial and Ethnic Disparities in Health Care. *Unequal Treatment: Confronting Racial and Ethnic Disparities in Health Care.* National Academies Press, 2003.

[24] Papanicolas, Irene, et al. "Association Between Wealth and Mortality in the United States and Europe." *New England Journal of Medicine*, vol. 392, 2 Apr. 2025, pp. 1310–1319, doi:10.1056/NEJMsa2408259. The study analyzed data from over 73,000 adults aged 50 to 85 across the U.S. and 16 European countries between 2010 and 2022.

[25] Pomerleau, Jonathan, et al. "Death Rates in England and Wales and the United States." *American Journal of Public Health*, vol. 94, no. 8, Aug. 2004, pp. 1367–1373. *PubMed Central*, https://www.ncbi.nlm.nih.gov/pmc/articles/PMC535447/. Research published in the *American Journal of Public Health* found that white Americans have significantly higher death rates than white individuals in England and Wales. Specifically, between the ages of 0 and 74, death rates for white U.S. males and females were 29% and 23% higher, respectively, than those for their counterparts in England and Wales. https://pmc.ncbi.nlm.nih.gov/articles/PMC535447.

Health is shaped less by what happens in hospitals and doctor's visits and more by living conditions, undue stress, and environmental factors.

Throughout the world, both industrialized and developing nations treat healthcare as a basic human right—accessible to all, not a benefit tied to employment.[26] Countries like the United Kingdom, Canada, France, and Japan provide universal healthcare through public systems, ensuring coverage regardless of job status, and many other nations do so as well. Even developing nations such as Thailand, Brazil, Colombia, and Rwanda have made significant strides toward affordable, inclusive healthcare. Also notable is Colombia, which provides universal healthcare coverage, treating healthcare as a fundamental human right. As of recent reports, approximately 99% of Colombia's population is covered by this system, making it one of the most comprehensive in Latin America.[27] The Colombian Constitution explicitly guarantees the right to health, stating that healthcare is a public service that must be provided under conditions of efficiency, universality, social solidarity, and participation. These nations mentioned are guided by the principle that healthcare is a

---

[26] World Health Organization. (1946). Constitution of the World Health Organization. World Health Organization. https://www.who.int/about/governance/constitution

[27] Ministerio de Salud y Protección Social. "Colombia Reached Universal Health Insurance at 99.6%." *Ministry of Health and Social Protection*, 29 June 2022, www.minsalud.gov.co/English/Paginas/Colombia-Reached-Universal-Health-Insurance-at-99.aspx.

universal right, and so healthcare access and affordability are extended beyond citizens to include foreigners.

These countries are not perfect and face challenges, yet the global trend is clear: healthcare is widely recognized as essential, not optional, and should be accessible to everyone. In contrast, the United States stands out among wealthy nations for linking health insurance primarily to employment and immigration status—leaving millions vulnerable. These nations—and many others—welcome foreign nationals, including Americans, into their healthcare systems without imposing exorbitant costs. This accessibility, often coupled with comprehensive coverage and quality care, makes such countries highly attractive destinations for expatriates seeking affordable, reliable healthcare abroad, and is especially crucial for retirees looking to move abroad.

Long-Term Care Facilities

If your decision to remain in the U.S. is based on the need for long-term care—whether for yourself or a loved one—rest assured that you can explore alternatives. Many countries offer long-term nursing homes that are not only significantly more affordable than those in the U.S. but also provide higher-quality facilities and medical care that rival the "best" facilities in the U.S.

Furthermore, relying solely on nursing home admissions in the U.S. is increasingly precarious. Nationwide, many nursing homes are closing due to rising construction and operational costs, and fewer new facilities are being built. Adding to the challenge, some nursing homes are being repurposed, leading to the eviction of residents. So, what was once a given—that seniors could count on receiving care in a nursing home—is becoming uncertain, forcing many to seek alternative care options. For this reason, it is wise to recognize that nursing homes may not be a viable, affordable, or reliable option for you or your loved ones soon.

Don't Have Much Saved for Retirement?

In addition to affordable healthcare, retirement abroad is especially attractive for those who were unable to save $500,000 or more. Rather, many countries allow you to retire comfortably on just your social security income. What a relief! So, if your retirement income is lean, there are many options available for you, such as Mexico, Colombia, Portugal, Malaysia, Thailand, and Vietnam. This is a short list, but if you do your research, there are many other possibilities.

The most important aspect of retirement abroad is figuring out your income and residency requirements. Once you know what you can afford based on daily living expenses such as rent, utilities, transportation, food, etc., you can narrow down where you should consider for your move abroad plan. Next, you want to figure out the residency requirements. Most countries allow U.S. passport holders to stay for 90 days without a visa. So, you can use this time to scout and see what life in another country will be like.

Next, you want to figure out your residency requirements. As a retiree, many countries allow you to become a resident as a "pension holder," which means you show that you have retirement income from the United States, and you will be permitted to stay legally. These are the most important factors when determining relocation because you want the legal right to remain in a country so you can optimize the social benefits that the country offers.

If you are curious about moving abroad and need some guidance, then I invite you to enroll in my course titled *Legally Abroad: An Attorney's Blueprint* for moving overseas, available here: https://www.accesswellnessglobal.com/moving-abroad-1.
Moving abroad is one of the most empowering adventures you can take; that is why I created this course to provide a step-by-step guide designed to give you everything you need to relocate with confidence. Here is what you will get inside:

⇒ **Practical Guidance** – Learn how to choose the right destination, navigate visa and residency processes, and understand the financial planning required for an international move.

⇒ **Cultural & Lifestyle Preparation** – From managing culture shock to building a new social circle. I will help you adapt and thrive in your new environment.

⇒ **Logistics Made Simple** – Housing, healthcare, banking, taxes, and insurance explained clearly, so you avoid costly mistakes.

⇒ **Career & Remote Work Strategies** – Whether you are transferring with a company, job hunting abroad, or working remotely, you will discover strategies to make your career transition smooth.

⇒ **Checklists, Templates & Resources** – Save time with ready-made planning tools to keep you organized every step of the way.

By the end of the course, you will not only feel prepared—you will be excited and empowered to start your new life abroad.

The takeaway is clear: for many, retiring in the U.S. is no longer a sustainable option. Rising costs, limited care facilities, and shrinking resources are pushing families to think beyond traditional plans. Exploring retirement abroad can offer more affordable living, higher-quality care, and a lifestyle that provides both dignity and security. By preparing ahead and considering international options, you can protect your loved ones from financial strain, avoid last-minute crises, and ensure that your retirement years are marked by stability, comfort, and peace of mind.

Final Thoughts

Estate planning is fundamental to achieving financial security for you and your family. Additionally, because people are experiencing financial insecurity, and there is so much political, social, and economic upheaval, I believe defaulting to the basics will help people feel more in control of their destiny. As an attorney, it has become abundantly clear that people can no longer afford to remain uninformed about the importance of estate planning and continue to delay getting to it.

In summary, from my perspective as an attorney, estate planning offers several key benefits:

(a) It serves as a valuable tax-saving tool.
(b) It educates the next generation on how to manage, leverage, and grow the assets they inherit.
(c) It can protect assets to help maintain Medicaid Long-Term Care eligibility.
(d) It ensures that the wealth created by one generation is preserved and used to build financial security for future generations.

Most importantly, through the example set by parents and grandparents who prepare estate plans, it sets up the succeeding generations to know how to be good stewards of assets. It is the blueprint for creating generational wealth because it can ensure that preceding generations leave assets to the next. So, even if you are not a multimillionaire, one of these topics is surely applicable to you. I hope that you take the first steps to ensure security for you and your family's future, and that you have now become more informed about the importance of estate planning.

Estate planning is not a one-time task. Life changes, and so should your plan. Marriage, divorce, the birth of a child, the death of a loved one, major financial changes, or even a shift in your personal values should prompt a review. It is wise to review your estate plan every two to three years or whenever a major life event occurs. Outdated documents can cause confusion or even legal disputes, so making updates a routine part of your life is a smart and responsible practice.

The information I provided does not replace your meeting with a licensed practitioner in your area, but can act as a guide to inform you as you take the next steps. This book invites you on a journey to thoughtfully plan for your future and safeguard the legacy you leave behind. By the end of this book, you should have the knowledge and confidence to build a solid plan that not only meets your personal needs but also provides peace of mind for you and your family.

Glossary of Terms

Advance Directives: a legal document that specifies a person's wishes regarding medical treatment if they become unable to communicate those decisions themselves.

Agent (under a Power of Attorney): a person authorized to act on behalf of another in financial or legal matters through a power of attorney document.

Beneficiary(ies): The people or organizations who receive money, property, or benefits from a will, trust, insurance policy, or other financial arrangement.

- ⇒ **Remainder Beneficiaries:** The people or entities who receive full ownership of a property or asset after the life tenant's interest ends—usually after the life tenant passes away.
- ⇒ **Beneficiary Designation:** the naming of a person or entity to receive assets directly from a retirement account, insurance policy, or other financial instruments upon the owner's death.
- ⇒ **Class of beneficiaries:** a group of individuals identified by a shared characteristic—such as "children" or "grandchildren"—who are entitled to benefit from a trust, Will, or insurance policy, without being named individually.

Codicil: a legal document that modifies or adds to an existing Will without replacing the entire Will.

Community Spouse Resource Allowance (CSRA): This is the portion of the couple's combined assets that the non-applicant spouse is allowed to retain. The CSRA is determined based on federal guidelines and varies by state.

Conservator: a person appointed by a court to manage the financial affairs and/or personal care of someone who is legally incapacitated or unable to manage their own affairs.

Countable assets (often called resources): are calculated toward Medicaid Long-Term Care's asset limit. This includes cash, stocks, bonds, investments, vacation homes, and bank accounts (i.e., checking, savings, and money market). There are also exempt (non-countable) assets.

Decedent: a legal term for a person who has died, particularly in the context of estate planning and probate law.

Disinherited: to be intentionally left out of a Will or denied a share of an inheritance by someone who would otherwise be expected to leave you assets upon their death (such as a parent, spouse, or child).

Distribution: the legal transfer of a person's assets to beneficiaries or heirs after their death, according to the terms of a Will, trust, or applicable state laws.

Disinterested parties: individuals or entities with no personal or financial stake in a legal matter or estate, often required to serve in impartial roles such as witnesses or court-appointed professionals.

Durable Power of Attorney: a power of attorney that remains effective even if the principal becomes incapacitated.

Estate: all the property, assets, and debts a person owns at the time of their death.

Estate tax: a tax imposed on the transfer of a deceased person's assets and property to their heirs or beneficiaries. It is calculated based on the total value of the estate before distribution, and only estates exceeding a certain exemption threshold are subject to this tax. The purpose of the estate tax is to generate revenue and, in some cases, to reduce the concentration of wealth passed between generations.

Executor: the person appointed in a Will to administer the deceased's estate according to the terms of the Will.

Exempt (or exemption): to be free from an obligation, duty, or liability that others are subject to. It indicates that a person, group, or item is not required to follow certain rules or regulations that typically apply.

Fiduciary: an individual or organization legally or ethically obligated to act in the best interests of another, typically in financial or trust-related matters.

Filial responsibility: legal obligations in some states requiring adult children to financially support their impoverished parents, including covering long-term care costs.

Funding a Trust: transferring ownership of an asset into the trust so that the trust—not an individual—legally holds those assets. This is a necessary step for the trust to function properly and carry out wishes.

Examples of Funding:

- ⇒ **Real estate**: Changing the deed to list the trust as the property owner.
- ⇒ **Bank accounts**: Retitling the account in the name of the trust.
- ⇒ **Investments or business interests**: Reassigning ownership to the trust.

Guardian: a person appointed by the court to care for and make decisions on behalf of a minor child or incapacitated adult.

Grantor: the individual who creates and funds a trust by transferring ownership of assets into it; also known as the settlor or trustor.

Gross Estate: the total value of everything a person owned or had certain interests in at the time of their death. Includes: real estate (homes, land), bank accounts, Investments (stocks, bonds), retirement accounts, life insurance (in some cases), personal property (cars, jewelry, art, etc., business interests.

Income: earnings generated by the trust's assets, not the assets themselves.

Inheritance Tax: a tax paid by beneficiaries on assets they inherit from a deceased person (differs from estate tax).

Intestacy law: the set of state laws that determine how a deceased person's estate is distributed when there is no valid Will.

Intestate or intestacy: the condition of dying without a valid Will, resulting in the estate being distributed under state intestacy laws.

Intestate Succession: the distribution of a deceased person's estate according to state law when no valid Will exists.

Joint Tenancy with Right of Survivorship: a form of property ownership where two or more people hold title jointly, and the surviving owner(s) automatically inherit the deceased owner's share.

Letters of Administration: court-issued documents that authorize a person to manage and distribute the estate of someone who died without a valid Will, including paying debts and distributing assets according to state law.

Life Estate: A legal arrangement where someone (called the "life tenant") has the right to use and live on a property for their lifetime. After they pass away, the property automatically goes to another person or group (called the "remainder beneficiaries")

Marital Deduction: a provision in U.S. tax law that allows a person to transfer unlimited assets to their spouse at death or during life without incurring federal estate or gift taxes, if the spouse is a U.S. citizen.

Medicaid Long-Term Care: a joint federal and state program that provides health coverage to eligible low-income individuals, including long-term care services.

Medicare (not to be confused with Medicaid Long-Term Care): a federal health insurance program primarily for individuals aged 65 and older, or younger individuals with certain disabilities or conditions.

Pass-through entity: a trust structure where income, deductions, and credits pass through the trust to the beneficiaries, who then report and pay tax on that income on their personal tax returns.

Petitioner of the Will: the person who submits a deceased individual's Will to the probate court to start the legal process of settling the estate. This person is typically a close relative, beneficiary, or the executor named in the Will. The petitioner's role is to request that the court validate the Will and grant them authority to manage the estate, ensuring assets are distributed according to the Will's instructions and outstanding debts or taxes are paid. Once approved, the petitioner—often officially appointed as the executor—takes on legal responsibility for administering the estate.

Penalty Divisor: the state's average monthly cost of private-pay nursing home care. Updated annually.

Penalty Period (in months): The amount of time Medicaid Long-term Care will penalize a Medicaid Long-Term Care applicant and not pay for Long-Term Care cost based on the calculation of Total Value of Assets Transferred ÷ State's Average Monthly Nursing Home Care Costs

Power of Attorney: a legal document authorizing someone to act on another's behalf in financial or medical matters.

Probate: the legal process of validating a deceased person's Will and overseeing the administration and distribution of their estate.

Settlor: the person who establishes a trust by transferring assets into it and defining its terms; also called a grantor or trustor.

Spending down (spend down): the process of reducing countable income or assets to meet Medicaid's financial limits.

Successor Trustee: the person or institution appointed to take over management of a trust when the original trustee (usually the person who created the trust) can no longer serve—due to death, incapacity, or resignation. They are responsible for managing, distributing, and protecting the trust's assets according to the instructions in the trust document.

⇒ The Successor Trustee steps in automatically without court approval if the trust is properly set up.

⇒ This role is similar to an executor of a Will, but for a trust—and it often avoids probate.

Step-Up Basis: is a tax rule that adjusts the value of an inherited asset—like a house or stocks—to its current market value at the time of the original owner's death. This new value becomes the starting point (basis) for calculating capital gains if the asset is later sold.

⇒ Step-up in basis is triggered by the owner's death, not by the legal method of transfer (trust vs. probate).
⇒ Whether the house passes to you through a revocable living trust, a Will, or intestate succession (no Will), the tax rule stays the same: the property gets a new cost basis equal to the fair market value on the date of death

Testator: a person who has made a legally valid Will outlining how their property should be distributed upon death.

Trusts (Revocable, Irrevocable, Special Needs):

⇒ **Revocable Trust:** a trust that can be modified or revoked by the grantor during their lifetime.
⇒ **Irrevocable Trust:** a trust that cannot be changed after it is established, used for purposes such as tax planning and Medicaid Long-Term Care eligibility.
⇒ **Special Needs Trust:** a trust designed to provide financial support to a person with disabilities without affecting their eligibility for government benefits.

Appendix A:
Sample Letter to Close Accounts

Re: Notice of Death of [Deceased's Name], Account Number: [Account Number]

Dear [Creditor's Name],

I am writing to formally notify you of the death of [Deceased's Full Name], who passed away on [Date of Death]. [He/She] was the account holder for the above-referenced account. I am [the executor of the estate/next of kin/authorized representative], and I am handling [his/her] affairs.

Please find enclosed a certified copy of the death certificate for your records.

I kindly request that you update your records to reflect [Deceased's Name]'s passing and stop any further correspondence to [his/her] name. Please let me know the process for closing the account and settling any outstanding balances. If the account has a balance due, I would appreciate it if you could provide a final statement with details regarding payment procedures. If any additional documentation or information is required, please feel free to contact me at [Your Phone Number] or [Your Email Address].

Thank you for your attention to this matter.

Sincerely,

[Your Full Name]
[Your Relationship to the Deceased]
[Enclosures: Death Certificate]

Appendix B:
Sample Letter to Decedent's Employer and/or Administrator

[Your Full Name]
[Your Address]
[City, State, ZIP Code]
[Phone Number]
[Email Address]

[Date]
[Employer or Pension Administrator Name]
[Company/Union Name]
[Company Address]
[City, State, ZIP Code]

RE: Notification of Death and Request for Final Employment and Pension Matters
Employee Name: [Full Name of Deceased]
Employee ID or SSN (last four digits): [XXX-XX-1234]

Dear [HR Manager / Pension Administrator / Union Representative],

I am writing to formally inform you of the passing of [Full Name of Deceased], who was employed with [Company Name] as a [Job Title] until [Date of Passing]. I am [his/her/their] [relation to the deceased—e.g., spouse, child, executor of the estate], and I am managing the necessary posthumous arrangements.

Enclosed with this letter is a **certified copy of the death certificate** for your records.

I respectfully request the following:

1. **Final Wages or Unpaid Compensation**
   Please provide any outstanding wages, vacation pay, or other compensation owed.

2. **Pension and Retirement Benefits**
   Kindly provide information about any retirement, pension, 401(k), or other benefits [he/she/they] may have been enrolled in, and the steps to claim any applicable survivor benefits

3. **Life Insurance (if applicable)**
   If [Company Name] offered life insurance coverage as part of its benefits, please forward the necessary claim forms and procedures to begin processing.

4. **Company Property**
   If there are any company-owned items (e.g., laptop, phone, ID badge, uniforms), please advise on how and where they should be returned.

Please send all necessary documentation and further instructions to the address listed above, or feel free to contact me at [Your Phone Number] or [Your Email Address] if further verification or documentation is needed.

Thank you for your attention to this sensitive matter. Your assistance during this difficult time is greatly appreciated.

Sincerely,
[Your Signature (if submitting a hard copy)]
[Your Printed Name]
[Relationship to the Deceased]
[Executor of the Estate, if applicable]

Appendix C:
Asset Preparation Worksheet

Use this worksheet to organize your assets and estate planning contacts. Keep it with your estate documents and update it regularly.

Personal Information

- Full Legal Name: _____
- Date of Birth: _____
- SSN (last 4 digits): XXX-XX-_____
- Home Address:_____
- Phone Number:_____
- Email Address:_____

Estate Planning Appointments

Trustee

- Full Name:_____
- Relationship to You:_____
- Phone Number:_____
- Email Address:_____
- Mailing Address:_____

Alternate Trustee (if primary cannot serve)

- Full Name:_____
- Relationship to You:_____
- Phone Number:_____
- Email Address:_____
- Mailing Address:_____

Executor of Will

- Full Name:_____
- Relationship to You:_____
- Phone Number:_____
- Email Address:_____
- Mailing Address:_____

Beneficiaries

(List all individuals or organizations you intend to name as beneficiaries in your estate plan.)

Full Name	Relationship	Phone Number	Email Address	Mailing Address

Real Estate Holdings

Property Type	Address	Ownership (Joint/Sole)	Estimated Value	Mortgage (Y/N)

Bank Accounts

Bank Name	Account Type (Checking/Savings)	Account # (last 4 digits)	Joint Owner? (Y/N)	Approximate Balance

Investment Accounts

Institution Name	Account Type (401k, IRA, etc.)	Account # (last 4 digits)	Approximate Balance	Named Beneficiary

Life Insurance Policies

Insurance Company	Policy Type (Term/Whole)	Policy Number	Death Benefit Amount	Beneficiary

Vehicles

Vehicle (Make/Model)	Year	Owner(s) on Title	Loan Balance	Location of Title

Digital Assets

Platform (e.g., Gmail, Crypto)	Type of Asset	Username or Email	Access Notes / Location

Valuable Personal Property or Collectibles

Description	Location	Estimated Value	Insured? (Y/N)

Business Interests

Business Name	Entity Type (LLC, Corp, etc.)	Ownership %	Estimated Value	Succession Plan Exists? (Y/N)

Important Legal Documents Checklist

Check all that apply and note where they are stored.

☐ Last Will and Testament – Stored:_____

☐ Living Trust – Stored:_____

☐ Power of Attorney – Stored:_____

☐ Health Care Proxy / Advance Directive – Stored:_____

☐ Property Deeds – Stored:_____

☐ Vehicle Titles – Stored:_____

☐ Marriage / Divorce Documents – Stored:_____

☐ Birth Certificates (self and children) – Stored:_____

☐ Insurance Policies – Stored:_____

☐ Recent Tax Returns – Stored:_____

☐ Military Records – Stored:_____

☐ Password List or Manager – Stored:_____

Safe Deposit Box or Home Safe

Do you have a bank safe deposit box? ☐ Yes / ☐ No

Bank Name and Location:_____

Key stored at:_____

Do you have a home safe? ☐ Yes / ☐ No

Location of safe:_____

Access code/password stored at:_____

NOTE: Review and update this worksheet at least once a year or when major life changes occur (birth, death, divorce, new assets, etc.). Keep copies secure and share with your appointed trustee, executor, or attorney as appropriate.

Free downloadable worksheets and letter templates are also available at www.accesswellnessglobal.com under the "Estate Planning for Expats" tab.

www.ingramcontent.com/pod-product-compliance
Lightning Source LLC
Chambersburg PA
CBHW070938180426
43192CB00039B/2322